1st EDITION

Perspectives on Diseases and Disorders

Fetal Alcohol Syndrome

Jacqueline Langwith
Book Editor

PERSPECTIVES
On Diseases & Disorders

GALE
CENGAGE Learning

Detroit • New York • San Francisco • New Haven, Conn • Waterville, Maine • London

Christine Nasso, *Publisher*
Elizabeth Des Chenes, *Managing Editor*

For more information, contact:
Greenhaven Press
27500 Drake Rd.
Farmington Hills, MI 48331-3535
Or you can visit our Internet site at gale.cengage.com

Articles in Greenhaven Press anthologies are often edited for length to meet page requirements. In addition, original titles of these works are changed to clearly present the main thesis and to explicitly indicate the author's opinion. Every effort is made to ensure that Greenhaven Press accurately reflects the original intent of the authors. Every effort has been made to trace the owners of copyrighted material.

Cover image © PhotoTake, Inc./Alamy

LIBRARY OF CONGRESS CATALOGING-IN-PUBLICATION DATA

Fetal alcohol syndrome / Jacqueline Langwith, book editor.
    p. cm. -- (Perspectives on diseases and disorders)
  Includes bibliographical references and index.
  ISBN 978-0-7377-4999-1 (hardcover)
  1. Fetal alcohol syndrome. I. Langwith, Jacqueline.
  RG629.F45F4613 2010
  618.3'26861--dc22

                                                           2010018199

Printed in the United States of America
1 2 3 4 5 6 7 14 13 12 11 10

CONTENTS

CHAPTER 1 Understanding Fetal Alcohol Syndrome

CHAPTER 3   Personal Experiences with
Fetal Alcohol Syndrome

FOREWORD

"Medicine, to produce health, has to examine disease."
—Plutarch

Independent research on a health issue is often the first step to complement discussions with a physician. But locating accurate, well-organized, understandable medical information can be a challenge. A simple Internet search on terms such as "cancer" or "diabetes," for example, returns an intimidating number of results. Sifting through the results can be daunting, particularly when some of the information is inconsistent or even contradictory. The Greenhaven Press series Perspectives on Diseases and Disorders offers a solution to the often overwhelming nature of researching diseases and disorders.

From the clinical to the personal, titles in the Perspectives on Diseases and Disorders series provide students and other researchers with authoritative, accessible information in unique anthologies that include basic information about the disease or disorder, controversial aspects of diagnosis and treatment, and first-person accounts of those impacted by the disease. The result is a well-rounded combination of primary and secondary sources that, together, provide the reader with a better understanding of the disease or disorder.

Each volume in Perspectives on Diseases and Disorders explores a particular disease or disorder in detail. Material for each volume is carefully selected from a wide range of sources, including encyclopedias, journals, newspapers, nonfiction books, speeches, government documents, pamphlets, organization newsletters, and position papers. Articles in the first chapter provide an authoritative, up-to-date overview that covers symptoms, causes and effects, treatments, cures, and medical advances. The second chapter presents a substantial number of opposing viewpoints on controversial treatments and other current debates relating to the volume topic. The third chapter offers a variety of personal perspectives on the disease or disorder. Patients, doctors, caregivers, and loved ones represent just some of the voices found in this narrative chapter.

Each Perspectives on Diseases and Disorders volume also includes:

- An **annotated table of contents** that provides a brief summary of each article in the volume.
- An **introduction** specific to the volume topic.
- Full-color **charts and graphs** to illustrate key points, concepts, and theories.
- Full-color **photos** that show aspects of the disease or disorder and enhance textual material.
- **"Fast Facts"** that highlight pertinent additional statistics and surprising points.
- A **glossary** providing users with definitions of important terms.
- A **chronology** of important dates relating to the disease or disorder.
- An annotated list of **organizations to contact** for students and other readers seeking additional information.
- A **bibliography** of additional books and periodicals for further research.
- A detailed **subject index** that allows readers to quickly find the information they need.

Whether a student researching a disorder, a patient recently diagnosed with a disease, or an individual who simply wants to learn more about a particular disease or disorder, a reader who turns to Perspectives on Diseases and Disorders will find a wealth of information in each volume that offers not only basic information, but also vigorous debate from multiple perspectives.

INTRODUCTION

In September 1999 The *Christian Science Monitor* introduced its readers to Anna Sinyaeva, a three-year-old orphan from Russia who likely has fetal alcohol syndrome (FAS). According to the *Monitor*, Anna was abandoned by her alcoholic mother at birth. Her medical records suggested signs of fetal alcohol syndrome. The doctor who examined her called her unresponsive and developmentally impaired. She ended up in a state-run orphanage outside Moscow. It was there at the age of three years that Anna Sinyaeva met Bob and Mary Rocklein from Massachusetts and became Hannah Faith Rocklein.

Hannah's story is not unique. According to UNICEF, the United Nations children's agency, more than one hundred thousand new orphans, mostly babies, are abandoned at Russian orphanages each year. Many of these babies are born to impoverished alcoholic mothers who drank during their pregnancy. Once the babies were born, the women, generally lacking resources and with other children at home, gave them up to the state. The precise number of children who have fetal alcohol spectrum disorders in Russian orphanages is unknown. However, experience and evidence suggest large numbers of Russian orphans suffer from the effects of prenatal alcohol exposure.

Drinking alcohol is deeply rooted in Russian culture. Each year Russians consume roughly 4.75 gallons of pure alcohol per person, more than double the level that the World Health Organization (WHO) considers a health threat and more than double the amount that Americans consume each year, according to a November 2009 story in the *New York Times*. Unlike other countries, where less potent beer and wine are more popular, Russians prefer hard liquors, such as vodka and whiskey. Vodka, the name of which comes from the Russian word for *water* (*voda*), constitutes the bulk of alcohol consumed in the country. In a speech made on August 12, 2009, Russian president Dmitry Medvedev lamented his country's alcohol problem: "You know just how serious a problem alcoholism has become for our country. Frankly speaking, it has taken on the proportions of a national disaster. According to the Healthcare and Social Development Ministry's statistics, per capita alcohol consumption in Russia—taking the whole population, including babies—now stands at 18 litres of pure alcohol a year. You can calculate for yourselves how many bottles of vodka this means—quite simply alarming."

Alexi Magalif, a doctor at a substance abuse clinic in Moscow, is worried about the pervasiveness of drinking in Russian society. In a September 2009 article in the *Christian Science Monitor*, Magalif is quoted as saying, "In our society, drinking has become the norm from top to bottom. Everyone drinks. No one drinks in moderation; they drink to get drunk, and it's overwhelming the medical system." Magalif's concerns are supported by a 2009 study published in the medical journal the *Lancet*, which found that alcohol was the cause of more than half of all Russian deaths between the ages of fifteen and fifty-four.

Scientists in Russia and across the world are studying the causes and effects of the country's high alcohol consumption rate. One group of researchers from the University of Oklahoma and the St. Petersburg State University in St. Petersburg, Russia, looked at the Russian public's awareness of the risks of maternal alcohol consumption. The researchers, Tatiana Balachova, Barbara Bonner, Galina Isurina, and Larissa Tsvetkova, surveyed men and women of reproductive age and Russian physicians about their knowledge of FAS. According to the researchers, most Russians are unaware of, or have misconceptions about, fetal alcohol disorders. For instance, many of them thought that a father who was drunk at the time of conception could affect a fetus. Additionally, the researchers found that most of the obstetricians and gynecologists in Russia demonstrated a lack of knowledge about FAS, inaccurately described the syndrome, or were unable to provide specific examples of FAS symptoms. Balachova and her associates noted that the participants in the study seemed to value the idea of a pregnant woman doing whatever she could to have a healthy baby; however, the "women and their partners paid disproportionately little attention to alcohol abstinence, and the need to stop drinking during pregnancy was not spontaneously mentioned as important for a baby's health." The researchers found that in general most Russians are uninformed about the potential harm posed by alcohol use during pregnancy.

Lack of information about FAS may account for the relatively large numbers of Russian orphans that appear to have been exposed to alcohol while in the womb. Studies have found that children at Russian orphanages have higher rates of fetal alcohol spectrum disorders than other children. Tufts University researcher Laurie Miller published a study in 2006 that found that a large number of babies in orphanages in the Murmansk region of Russia exhibited facial features and other physical anomalies that suggested fetal alcohol exposure. In another study, researchers at the University of Minnesota's International Adoption Center evaluated children adopted from China, Guatemala, Korea, Russia, and several eastern European countries. Only the children from eastern Europe and Russia had classifiable fetal alcohol spectrum disorders (FASD). Of these, Russia alone accounted for 79 percent of the children and 85 percent of the FASD diagnoses. According to Tatiana Balachova and her associates, these and other findings indicate that the rate of FAS in children from Russian orphanages may be "as high as 53 to 145 per 1,000 children." This is nearly thirty times higher than the reported worldwide incidence rate of 1.9 per 1,000 live births.

Some children adopted from Russian orphanages receive an official diagnosis of fetal alcohol syndrome when they come to the United States, while others do not. Hannah Rocklein never received a diagnosis of FAS or any other alcohol-related disorder. When she first came home, her American physicians noted that she seemed a bit behind in her mental and motor development skills, but otherwise she was "absolutely healthy." For another child—Katia Demchuck—adopted a year before Hannah in 1998, the situation was different. According to a story

Russian schoolchildren view an exhibition of deformed fetuses as they learn about the dangers of fetal alcohol syndrome, a condition that is prevalent in their country. (Dima Korotayev/Reuters/Landov)

from the Web site Cleveland.com, Katia's adoptive parents immediately knew she had FAS when they adopted her. According to Katia's adoptive mother, Felicia, "We recognized the facial characteristics of fetal alcohol syndrome right away. But it didn't matter. We just knew she had to be with us." In 2008 an eleven-year-old Katia Demchuk spoke before the U.S. Congress on the need to raise awareness about early intervention and diagnosis of FAS. Katia told Congress how difficult it is for her to read, write, and remember math facts. Katia's mother also told Congress of the necessity of raising awareness about the importance of not drinking alcohol during pregnancy.

In *Perspectives on Diseases and Disorders: Fetal Alcohol Syndrome*, the contributors provide an overview of what scientists know about FAS, its causes and its treatments, and how it affects people like Hannah and Katia. They also provide differing viewpoints on certain controversial issues surrounding FAS and personal accounts of living with the effects of prenatal alcohol exposure.

CHAPTER 1

Understanding Fetal Alcohol Syndrome

An Overview of Fetal Alcohol Syndrome

Laurie Heron Seaver, Teresa G. Odle, and Tish Davidson

In the following article Laurie Heron Seaver, Teresa G. Odle, and Tish Davidson discuss fetal alcohol syndrome. According to the authors, fetal alcohol syndrome (FAS) is the most severe form of a range of disorders, referred to as fetal alcohol spectrum disorder (FASD), affecting individuals whose mothers drank alcohol during pregnancy. Classic features of FAS include short stature, low birth weight, poor weight gain, a distinct pattern of facial abnormalities, and varying degrees of mental retardation. The authors say there is no cure for FAS and nothing can change the physical features or brain damage caused by maternal drinking. However, early diagnosis and stable and nurturing home environments have been found to reduce the risk of learning and behavioral disabilities. Seaver, Odle, and Davidson are nationally published medical writers.

Photo on facing page. Mothers who drink alcohol during pregnancy run a high risk of having children with FAS. (© Graham Dunn/Alamy)

SOURCE: Laurie Heron Seaver, Teresa G. Odle, and Tish Davidson, *A.M. Gale Encyclopedia of Medicine*. Belmont, CA: Gale, 2007. Copyright © 2007 by Gale. Reproduced by permission of Gale, a part of Cengage Learning.

F AS [Fetal Alcohol Syndrome] is the most severe of a range of disorders represented by the term fetal alcohol spectrum disorder (FASD). FAS/FASD is caused by exposure of a developing fetus to alcohol. FASD is used to describe individuals with some, but not all, of the features of FAS. Other terms used to describe specific types of FASD are alcohol-related neurodevelopmental disorder (ARND) and alcohol-related birth defects (ARBD).

The Most Common Preventable Cause of Mental Retardation

FAS is the most common preventable cause of mental retardation. This condition was first recognized and reported in the medical literature in 1968 in France and in 1973 in the United States. Alcohol is a teratogen, the term used for any drug, chemical, maternal disease, or other environmental exposure that can cause birth defects or functional impairment in a developing fetus. Some features of FAS may be present at birth, including low birth weight, prematurity, and microcephaly [small or underdeveloped skull]. Characteristic facial features may be present at birth, or may become more obvious over time. Signs of brain damage include delays in development, behavioral abnormalities, and mental retardation, but affected individuals exhibit a wide range of abilities and disabilities.

FAS is not curable, and has long-term consequences. Learning, behavioral, and emotional problems are common in adolescents and adults with FAS. The costs of FAS to the American economy were estimated in 2006 as [$]321 million annually.

The incidence of FAS varies among different populations studied, depending on the degree of alcohol use within the population and ranges from approximately 0.2 to 1.5 in every 1,000 births in the United States. FAS/FASD is independent of any racial or ethnic inheritance. Instead, the incidence of FASD is directly related to how much

alcohol a woman drinks while she is pregnant. FAS/FASD is 100% preventable by avoiding alcohol during the entire pregnancy, including the earliest weeks. No amount of alcohol use during pregnancy has been proven to be completely safe.

The symptoms of FAS include facial abnormalities, short stature, low birth weight, and mental retardation. (© Golden Pixels LLC/ Alamy)

The risk of FAS appears to increase as a woman with chronic alcoholism ages. Often the child with FAS will be one of the last born to a woman with chronic alcoholism, although older siblings may exhibit milder features of FASD. Binge drinking, defined as sporadic use of five or more standard alcoholic drinks per occasion, and "moderate" daily drinking (two to four 12 oz. bottles of beer, eight to 16 ounces of wine, two to four ounces of liquor) can also result in children with FASD. Some experts believe that a few binges at critical times early in pregnancy —possibly even before a woman may know she is pregnant

—may be enough to cause FASD even if the woman stops drinking later in pregnancy.

Alcohol Is Damaging to the Developing Fetus

The only cause of FAS is maternal use of alcohol during pregnancy. FAS is not a genetic or inherited disorder. Alcohol drunk by the mother freely crosses the placenta and damages the developing fetus. Alcohol use by the father cannot cause FAS. Not all offspring who are exposed to alcohol during pregnancy have signs or symptoms of FAS; individuals of different genetic backgrounds may be more or less susceptible to the damage that alcohol can cause. The amount of alcohol, stage of development of the fetus, and the pattern of alcohol use create the range of symptoms that encompass FASD.

Classic features of FAS include short stature, low birth weight, poor weight gain, microcephaly, and a characteristic pattern of abnormal facial features. These facial features

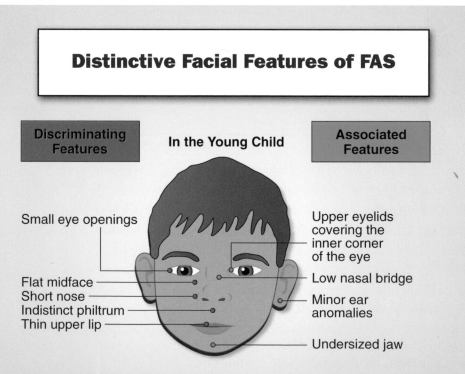

Distinctive Facial Features of FAS

Discriminating Features	In the Young Child	Associated Features

Small eye openings

Flat midface
Short nose
Indistinct philtrum
Thin upper lip

Upper eyelids covering the inner corner of the eye

Low nasal bridge

Minor ear anomalies

Undersized jaw

Taken from: National Institute on Alcohol Abuse and Alcoholism.

in infants and children may include small eye openings (measured from inner corner to outer corner), epicanthal folds (folds of tissue at the inner corner of the eye), small or short nose, low or flat nasal bridge, smooth or poorly developed philtrum (the area of the upper lip above the colored part of the lip and below the nose), thin upper lip, and small chin. Some of these features are nonspecific, meaning they can occur in other conditions, or be appropriate for age, racial, or family background.

Other major and minor birth defects that have been reported with FASD include cleft palate, congenital heart defects, strabismus [unaligned eyes], hearing loss, defects of the spine and joints, alteration of the hand creases, small fingernails, and toenails. Since FAS was first described in infants and children, the diagnosis is sometimes more difficult to recognize in older adolescents and adults. Short stature and microcephaly remain common features, but weight may normalize, and the individual may actually become overweight for his/her height. The chin and nose grow proportionately more than the middle part of the face, and dental crowding may become a problem. The small eye openings and the appearance of the upper lip and philtrum may continue to be characteristic. Pubertal changes typically occur at the normal time.

Newborns with FAS may have difficulty nursing due to a poor sucking response, have irregular sleep-wake cycles, decreased or increased muscle tone, seizures or tremors. Delays in achieving developmental milestones such as rolling over, crawling, walking, and talking may become apparent in infancy. Behavior and learning difficulties typical in the preschool or early school years include poor attention span, hyperactivity, poor motor skills, and slow language development. Attention deficit-hyperactivity disorder (ADHD) is often associated with FASD. Learning disabilities or mental retardation may be diagnosed during this time.

During middle school and high school years the behavioral difficulties and learning difficulties can be significant. Memory problems, poor judgment, difficulties with daily living skills, difficulties with abstract reasoning skills, and poor social skills are often apparent by this time. It is important to note that animal and human studies have shown that neurologic and behavioral abnormalities can be present without characteristic facial features. These individuals may not be identified as having FAS, but may fulfill criteria for alcohol-related neurodevelopmental disorder (ARND).

FASD continues to affect individuals into adulthood. One study looked at FAS adults and found that about 95% had mental health problems, 82% lacked the ability to live independently, 70% had problems staying employed, 60% had been in trouble with the law, and 50% of men and 70% of women were alcohol or drug abusers.

Another long-term study found that the average IQ of the group of adolescents and adults with FAS in the study was 68 (70 is lower limit of the normal range). However, the range of IQ was quite large, ranging from a low of 20 (severely retarded) to a high of 105 (normal). Academic abilities and social skills were also below normal levels.

Diagnosis, Treatment, and Prevention

The diagnosis of FAS is made based on the history of maternal alcohol use and detailed physical examination for the characteristic major and minor birth defects and facial features. There are no blood, X-ray, or psychological tests that will confirm the suspected diagnosis. Sometimes genetic tests are performed to rule out other conditions that may present with similar developmental delays or birth defects. Psychoeducational testing to determine IQ and/or the presence of learning disabilities may also be part of the evaluation process.

There is no cure for FAS. The disorder is irreversible. Nothing can change the physical features or brain damage associated with maternal alcohol use during the pregnancy. Children should have psychoeducational evaluation to help plan appropriate educational interventions. Common associated diagnoses such as ADHD, depression, or anxiety can be recognized and treated. The disabilities that present during childhood persist into adult life. However, some of the behavioral problems mentioned above may be avoided or lessened by early and correct diagnosis, better understanding of the life-long complications of FAS, and intervention. The goal of treatment is to help the individual affected by FAS become as independent and successful in school, employment, and social relationships as possible. . . .

The prognosis for FAS depends on the severity of birth defects and the brain damage present at birth. Miscarriage, stillbirth, or death in the first few weeks of life may be outcomes in very severe cases. Some physical birth defects associated with FAS are treatable with surgery. Some of the factors that have been found to reduce the risk of learning and behavioral disabilities in FAS individuals include diagnosis before the age of six years, stable and nurturing home environments, never having experienced personal violence, and referral and eligibility for disability services. The long-term data helps in understanding the difficulties that individuals with FAS encounter throughout

FAST FACT

According to the Centers for Disease Control and Prevention, scientists believe that there are at least three times as many cases of FASD as FAS.

their lifetime and can help families, caregivers, and professionals provide the care, supervision, education, and treatment geared toward their special needs.

FAS is completely preventable by avoiding all alcohol during pregnancy. Prevention efforts include public education efforts aimed at the entire population, not just women of child bearing age, appropriate treatment for women with high-risk drinking habits, and increased recognition and knowledge about FAS/FASD by professionals, parents, and caregivers.

Genes May Determine Sensitivity to Maternal Alcohol Exposure

Science Daily

In the following article *Science Daily* discusses research results that suggest a link between a serotonin-regulating gene and fetal alcohol syndrome (FAS). Scientists studying alcohol's effects on rhesus monkeys found that monkeys that carry a shortened form of a gene that regulates the neurotransmitter serotonin were more likely to be affected by maternal alcohol consumption than monkeys that have the longer form of the gene. The research may explain why some babies exposed to alcohol in the womb are unharmed while others suffer from FAS. According to *Science Daily*, researchers are also looking for other genes that may be linked to FAS and hope to use the information to identify and help vulnerable children who may have been exposed to alcohol during prenatal development. *Science Daily* is an Internet Web site providing news stories on the latest scientific breakthroughs.

SOURCE: Madeline Fisher, "Study Reveals Possible Genetic Risk For Fetal Alcohol Disorders," *University of Wisconsin–Madison, School of Education Online News,* September 21, 2007. Copyright © 2007 Board of Regents of the University of Wisconsin System. Reproduced by permission.

New research in primates suggests that infants and children who carry a certain gene variant may be more vulnerable to the ill effects of fetal alcohol exposure.

Reported Sept. 21 [2007] in *Biological Psychiatry*, the findings represent the first evidence of a genetic risk for fetal alcohol spectrum disorder—a condition that is characterized by profound mental retardation in its most severe form, but which is also associated with deficits in learning, attention, memory and impulse control.

By identifying a genetic marker that might signal susceptibility to these more subtle fetal alcohol-induced problems, the research fills a pressing need, says Mary Schneider, the University of Wisconsin–Madison [UW–Madison]professor of kinesiology and psychology who led the study.

"The big concern used to be the link between fetal alcohol exposure and mental retardation, but today there is increased concern over behavioral problems in these children," says Schneider. "If this genetic marker could provide a way of recognizing the most vulnerable fetal alcohol-exposed children early in life, perhaps we could help them to live more successful and satisfying lives."

The study's results may also help to explain why some children of mothers who drink during pregnancy suffer birth defects, while others seem to escape unharmed.

"Children who are exposed to alcohol because their mothers drank during pregnancy have varying degrees of problems, and the same is true for monkeys who are exposed to moderate levels of alcohol in utero," says Schneider. "So we know there are other factors involved."

Investigating a Serotonin-Regulating Gene

With colleagues at UW–Madison, the University of Toronto and the National Institutes of Health, Schneider

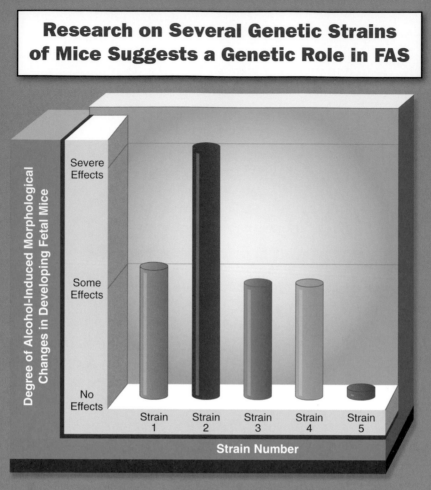

Research on Several Genetic Strains of Mice Suggests a Genetic Role in FAS

Degree of Alcohol-Induced Morphological Changes in Developing Fetal Mice

Severe Effects

Some Effects

No Effects

Strain 1 — Strain 2 — Strain 3 — Strain 4 — Strain 5

Strain Number

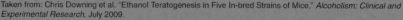

Taken from: Chris Downing et al. "Ethanol Teratogenesis in Five In-bred Strains of Mice," *Alcoholism: Clinical and Experimental Research*, July 2009.

investigated two forms of a gene called the serotonin transporter gene promoter, which helps regulate the brain chemical serotonin. Past studies of both people and primates suggest that carriers of a short form of this gene are at increased risk for depression, but only if they also experience adverse life events.

To test whether the gene's short form might also raise the risk of fetal alcohol-induced problems, Schneider's team analyzed data from an ongoing, long-term study into the impacts of moderate fetal alcohol exposure on behavior and brain function in rhesus monkeys. Although fetal alcohol syndrome was first recognized in children of alcoholic mothers, attention has shifted in recent years to moderate drinking because of its potential to affect many more children, says Schneider.

"We know that 60 percent of women of child-bearing age consume alcohol and more than 50 percent of pregnancies are unplanned," she says. "So it doesn't take much to figure out that prenatal exposure to alcohol—at least in the weeks before pregnancy is detected—is substantial."

In line with this, the mother monkeys in the study's experimental group consumed the equivalent of just two alcoholic beverages five times a week during breeding and pregnancy. After the infants were born, the scientists recorded their irritability during a standard battery of developmental tests, measured their reactivity to stress when separated from their mothers at six months for weaning, and determined whether they carried the short or long form of the serotonin transporter gene promoter.

Short Form Gene Carriers More Susceptible

What the researchers found is that fetal alcohol-exposed infants who carried a copy of the short form were more irritable and reactive to stress than either control group infants who weren't exposed to alcohol or those who were exposed but had two copies of the gene's long form. Overall, says Schneider, the results indicate a "substantial interaction" between fetal alcohol exposure and genotype.

She and her colleagues are now conducting additional studies to see if these findings fit a larger pattern of fetal alcohol-induced problems as the monkeys grow up. At the same time, extreme irritability and stress responsiveness in infants can themselves lead to problems, she says.

"If a baby is very irritable and stress reactive, one of the things this can interfere with is the caregiver-infant

> **FAST FACT**
>
> According to the Substance Abuse and Mental Health Services Administration, fetal alcohol spectrum disorders affect nearly forty thousand newborns each year.

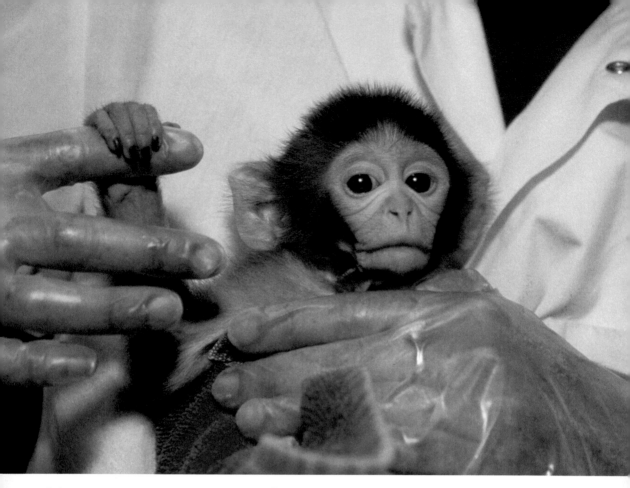

Scientists researching the effects of alcohol on rhesus monkeys in utero found that genotype, or the genetic makeup of an organism, interacts with fetal alcohol exposure, contributing to the development of FAS. (Richard T. Nowitz/Photo Researchers, Inc.)

interaction," she says. "In real life, negative events tend to cluster. So if there's alcohol in the environment, there may also be stress. And then if you have an irritable baby, this all could have cascading effects on the child's psychological development."

Recognizing that complex behaviors are seldom, if ever, governed by a single gene, Schneider and her colleagues are also investigating other gene alleles for their potential to interact with fetal-alcohol exposure and put children at risk.

"Genetics by themselves rarely tell us much, because life experiences may trigger the actual effects of our genetic vulnerabilities," says Schneider. "So the more knowledge we have about the ways that genes interact with environmental factors, the more we can envision interventions early in life to help a vulnerable child."

A Certain B Vitamin May Prevent FAS

PLoS Medicine

In the following article *PLoS Medicine* discusses the research results of Cornell University scientists who found that a common B vitamin can reverse many of the damaging effects of alcohol on developing fetuses. The scientists used mice as models to see whether administering nicotinamide, a form of vitamin B_3, a few hours after alcohol exposure could prevent or reverse some of the brain damage caused when developing fetuses are exposed to alcohol. According to the author, the researchers found that a small dose of nicotinamide administered two hours after alcohol exposure helped keep fetal mouse brain cells from dying and reduced the amount of behavioral abnormalities exhibited by the mice after they were born. *PLoS Medicine* is an open-access scientific journal published on the Internet by the Public Library of Science.

The most common cause of nongenetic mental retardation in the Western world is fetal alcohol syndrome (FAS). About one in 1,000 United States

SOURCE: *PLoS Medicine*, "Nicotinamide: A Way to Prevent Fetal Alcohol Syndrome?" vol. 3, April 2006. Copyright © 2006 Public Library of Science. Reproduced by permission.

children is born with FAS, which is caused by prenatal exposure to alcohol. Children with FAS typically have abnormal facial features and reduced growth. They also have central nervous system abnormalities that lead to impaired learning and memory skills, hyperactivity, and other behavioral problems. These neurological disabilities arise because ethanol disrupts the formation and survival of neurons in the developing brain, particularly in the last trimester of pregnancy and in the first few years of postnatal life when brain development is particularly active.

Nicotinamide May Protect Fetuses

There is no cure for FAS, but it is 100% preventable. Public health officials recommend that women planning pregnancy and sexually active women who do not use effective birth control avoid alcohol—there is no safe dose of alcohol or safe time to drink it during pregnancy. Sadly, this advice is often ignored. In the US, one in 12 pregnant women admits to drinking alcohol, and one in 30 reports binge drinking (five or more drinks at one time). Given such figures, ways to prevent or attenuate the effects of alcohol on the developing brain are badly needed. Alessandro Ieraci and Daniel Herrera now report that nicotinamide (the amide form of vitamin B_3) can prevent some of the deleterious effects of ethanol on developing mice brains, and suggest that nicotinamide might be suitable as a preventative therapy for FAS.

Nicotinamide is the precursor of β-nicotinamide adenine dinucleotide, which enhances the action of many enzymes and is therefore essential for cellular function. Nicotinamide and other forms of vitamin B_3 have been used for many years as dietary supplements to treat and prevent pellagra, a vitamin deficiency disease. Large oral doses of nicotinamide have also been used over extended periods of time in clinical trials to treat type I diabetes and bullous pemphigoid (a chronic, autoimmune skin-blistering disease). In addition, recent animal data indicate that nicotinamide is also neuroprotective. In rat models of stroke, for example, it improves neurological outcomes by inhibiting the neuronal apoptosis caused by oxygen deprivation. In apoptosis (a highly organized form of cell death), mitochondrial breakdown releases the protein cytochrome-c, which activates enzymes known as initiator caspases. These activate effector caspases (including caspase-3), which digest other cellular substrates and kill the cell without releasing any potentially harmful molecules. Nicotinamide acts as a neuroprotectant in part by inhibiting cytochrome-c release and caspase-3 activation.

> **FAST FACT**
>
> According to the American College of Obstetricians and Gynecologists, part of the reason alcohol is so harmful to fetuses is that the liver of a developing fetus is not yet able to break it down.

As induction of apoptosis is one known mechanism by which ethanol harms neurons, Ieraci and Herrera asked whether nicotinamide could reduce the effects of ethanol in a mouse model of FAS. Subcutaneous injection of ethanol triggers widespread neurodegeneration in seven-day-old mice—whose brain development is comparable to that of human fetuses in the third trimester of pregnancy. The researchers report that an ethanol injection sufficient to raise blood ethanol levels to those that a human fetus would be exposed to if its mother indulged in binge-like drinking activated caspase-3 and induced the release of cytochrome-c. They then show that nicotinamide injected up to eight hours after the ethanol reduced caspase-3 activation and cytochrome-c release without altering blood or brain ethanol levels.

Nicotinamide Reversed Damage to Brain

As the "normalizing" effects of nicotinamide were strongest when it was administered zero to two hours after alcohol exposure, Ieraci and Herrera next investigated

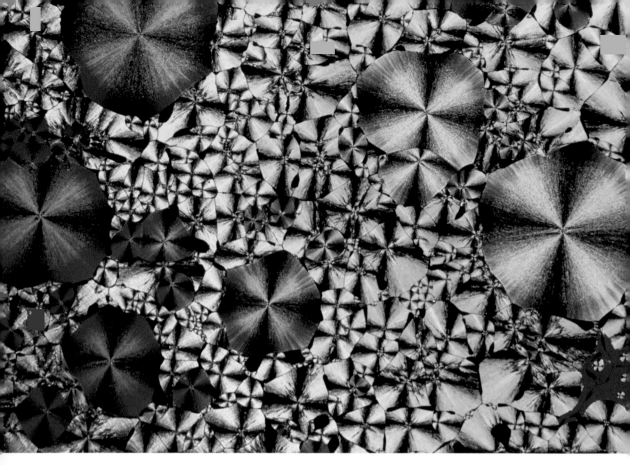

A polarized light micrograph shows nicotinamide crystals. Research has shown that nicotinamide can reverse some of the fetal brain damage caused by a mother's alcohol abuse. (Sidney Moulds/Photo Researchers, Inc.)

whether nicotinamide given two hours after alcohol injection could prevent ethanol-induced neuronal death. To look for early signs of neuronal injury, they stained brain sections with Fluoro-Jade B soon after exposing the mice to ethanol. Most damage occurred in brain regions particularly sensitive to ethanol at this age—namely, the anterior cingulate cortex (which is involved in cognition), the hippocampus (a region needed for learning and memory), and the thalamus (which relays messages from the outside world to other brain regions); nicotinamide treatment reduced this damage. When the researchers stained brain sections for NeuN, a marker of mature neurons, several days after ethanol exposure, they found reduced numbers of neurons (compared with control brains) in similar brain regions, and, again, nicotinamide treatment reduced ethanol's effects. Finally, the researchers used three standard behavioral assays to test whether the reduction in

ethanol-induced neuronal death produced by nicotinamide affected the behavior of adult mice. They report
that nicotinamide reversed the increase in hyperactivity
and the decrease in fear caused by ethanol exposure, and
prevented the impairment in learning and memory induced by ethanol.

In mice, then, these results show that nicotinamide can
reverse the molecular, cellular, and behavioral effects of
ethanol exposure on developing brains. While the beneficial effects observed were most pronounced when nicotinamide was given at the same time or shortly after alcohol
exposure, the study suggests that there is a time window of
a few hours during which treatment with nicotinamide
might be effective. More studies are needed to determine
exactly how nicotinamide protects neurons against alcohol
-induced damage, but the data raise the possibility that
nicotinamide treatment may provide a way to prevent
some human cases of FAS.

Adults with FAS Face Challenges

Tom Robertson

In the following article Tom Robertson illuminates the difficulties faced by adults who are brain damaged as a result of fetal alcohol exposure. Robertson says adults with fetal alcohol spectrum disorder (FASD) are disorganized, unpredictable, and have a hard time taking care of themselves. Since their disability is often invisible, Robertson says, the social safety nets that exist for other disabilities are generally unavailable. Adults with FASD, however, are living productive, meaningful lives with the help of family, friends, employers, and organizations devoted to helping them cope with their disability. Robertson is a reporter and producer for Minnesota Public Radio.

There are very few places in the country that specialize in residential care for adults with fetal alcohol brain damage. That's what makes Westbrook farm west of Duluth [Minnesota] so unique.

It's a gorgeous setting—160 acres of rolling pastures and thick forests near the St. Louis River. The farm is home to

SOURCE: Tom Robertson, "Adults with Fetal Alcohol Syndrome Face Huge Challenges," Minnesota Public Radio, November 21, 2007. Copyright © 2007 Minnesota Public Radio. All rights reserved. Reproduced by permission.

eight young men struggling with the lasting effects of pre-natal alcohol exposure.

Without the Farm, He Would Be in Prison

Two brown and white miniature horses nibble hay in the barn. Billy Nelson, 20, gently scratches their ears. Nelson considers the horses his friends—and his therapy.

"This one's Drummer and that one's Chance," says Nelson. "You can take them out in the yard and run with them, and they stay by your side. They're really nice horses."

Nelson has lived at Westbrook for about two years, but it was a rough road getting here. His mom was a drinker. He and his twin brother were born in St. Paul three and a half months premature. His brother died just a few weeks after birth.

Nelson was placed in a series of foster homes, treatment centers and psychiatric care facilities. He was into drugs and alcohol, and was prone to violence. Nelson figures if he hadn't ended up at this farm, he'd probably be in prison.

"I used to be crazy and all that when I first came here, but then I realized what my plan was to do on this earth before I pass on," says Nelson. "I need to take the punches and say, hey, just get my stuff together so I can move on in life and better myself. Because if you don't better yourself, you're not going nowhere."

Westbrook farm was started [in 2002] by a Duluth non-profit organization called Residential Services, Inc. The goal is to teach basic living skills to adults affected by fetal alcohol exposure, and help them live independently.

It's a population that health advocates say is grossly underserved in this country. Studies show 90 percent have mental health problems, and 80 percent have trouble holding onto a job.

Each Day Is Unpredictable

Nelson and the others at Westbrook lack impulse control and have trouble understanding the consequences of their behaviors.

Travis Dombrovski, manager of Westbrook, says that means daily life on the farm is unpredictable and sometimes explosive.

"They break things, and they yell and they scream and they swear, and they're hyper-sexual," Dombrovski says. "Assaults, sure, phones being thrown, lots of property destruction. It's got to be a helpless feeling. It's got to be scary and it's got to be hard to understand."

Dombrovski says Westbrook's residents have trouble learning from their mistakes, so instead of punishment, they face what he calls "natural consequences." For example, when someone gets angry and breaks something, they're required to fix or replace it.

Despite evidence that punishment is ineffective on adults affected by fetal alcohol, some 60 percent of them will spend time behind bars. Dombrovski say society needs to take a different approach.

"They don't need to be in jail. Jail is not the right place," says Dombrovski. "Sure, there might be structure, but there's no learning, there's no help, there's no support. And it's a waste of a human life, in my opinion, to leave them in jail. They can come out. They can make it."

There's typically a long waiting list to get into Westbrook. Residents are usually referred there by county social service agencies, which pay the costs through foster care and other program funds.

The residents start out living in the main farmhouse, where life is highly structured. They're assigned daily chores. They learn how to cook and clean and take care of themselves. They tend to the farm animals and work in the garden.

Then, when they're ready, they can graduate to more independent living in an apartment building just across the yard.

Billy Nelson says he's ready to move into one of those apartments. For the first time in his life, he's set some goals for himself. He wants to earn his GED, and would someday like to study climatology. Nelson says Westbrook has given him a confidence he's never had before.

"Trust was a big issue when I first came here," says Nelson. "I didn't trust no one. Not even myself. Didn't believe in myself. But now I do believe in myself. And I know I can do whatever I want to, as long as I put my head to it."

No Safety Net for Adults

Helping alcohol-exposed children grow into adults can be a nightmare for parents. Jodee Kulp lives in a western Twin Cities suburb, where she and her husband raised their adopted daughter, Liz, who's now 21 years old.

Kulp says people with more visible disabilities have clear safety nets, but for young adults with fetal alcohol syndrome, getting help can be a struggle.

Adults with FAS are plagued with behavior problems. (Bill Roth/MCT/Landov)

"The rule is, fail first. And failing first is very painful," says Kulp. "It's very painful as a parent to watch your child fail. It's very painful to watch your child fail over and over and over again."

Like many people with fetal alcohol brain damage, Liz has trouble managing her money. She's gone into treatment twice for alcohol abuse. Liz says when she first moved out on her own at age 18, one of her biggest problems was housing. She says people took advantage of her.

"I had basically a party house where friends wouldn't leave," Liz says. "By me just inviting maybe one person, they invite whoever else. But they wouldn't leave and then I didn't know what to do, and eventually got kicked out of a lot of apartments."

In all, Liz was booted from nine apartments in just two years. Her mother says Liz tried to do the right thing, but just wasn't capable.

"For a long time, I felt like I was swimming in the sharks, running around from place to place trying to save her and help her, and try to teach her and help her learn," says Jodee Kulp. "And then finally you look at the situation and say, you know what, in order for her to get services, I've just got to let her fail. And then you just go on your knees, because that's the only option you've got is to just let it happen."

Kulp's daughter eventually qualified for disability services. Liz gets financial help with her rent. The county provides Liz with a job coach to help her find work. She's managed to keep the same apartment for almost a year.

Liz says she still struggles just to contain her emotions. She says little things will irritate her and she can feel the anger welling up in her body. Sometimes it turns into a meltdown, and Liz says things she doesn't mean.

"I can get out of hand. I've calmed down a little bit, but I tend to break things," says Liz. "And people all turn their head and I get frustrated and I yell at them all, because I don't like it when people stare me down. It frustrates me, because they look at me like I'm crazy or something. It's just that I'm frustrated and I don't know how to maintain, and I'm just like, breaking out of my own skin."

Jodee Kulp quit her job years ago to devote her life to helping Liz succeed. She helped Liz write a book about what it's like to live with fetal alcohol damage. Liz is now working on a second book focusing on the challenges of making the transition to adult life. Jodee and Liz work together to raise awareness of the disorder.

"The first thing we need to do is we need to change our frame of reference, which is realizing they have a brain injury," says Jodee Kulp. "Once we understand that we're dealing with a brain injury, we start working with the population in a different way. . . . The idea is to build a national voice for persons with fetal alcohol."

What's most difficult for Liz's dad, Karl Kulp, is to not blame Liz for her bad behavior. Karl says he still has to remind himself that Liz can't help it because her brain is damaged.

Karl says the future is too far ahead to even consider that Liz could someday become a productive adult.

"We're immensely gratified that Liz is alive at 21," Karl says. "There were so many ways, and there have been so many instances along the way, where it could have gone the other way and she may not have survived. And it isn't clear yet whether she's going to make 22. She just doesn't have the brain function to guide herself in the right way all the time. So she makes a lot more mistakes."

Making It Work—with Help from Others

Some adults with fetal alcohol damage are doing their best to lead productive lives. Monica Adams is assistant manager of a women's clothing store in a Twin Cities suburb.

"Is there anything I can get for anyone?" says Adams to several customers. "Just looking? OK. If you have any questions, don't hesitate to ask."

Adams, 37, has gone through two failed marriages. Now she's moved back in with her adoptive parents.

Adams says she struggled all her life to fit in and understand the world around her. She sucked her thumb habitually until fifth grade. She had no concept of money or time, and school was always frustrating.

"A lot of things I just flat out didn't understand," says Adams. "I mean, a teacher would be talking and I'm like, what in the world is coming out of her mouth? Everybody else seemed to know. I was always the 'day late' person, always asking the person next to me. I feel like I got more of an education adapting to my surroundings than I ever did learning the ABCs, because I had to."

Adams says she's learned to adapt to her disability with strong support from family, friends and an employer who's willing to put up with her faults.

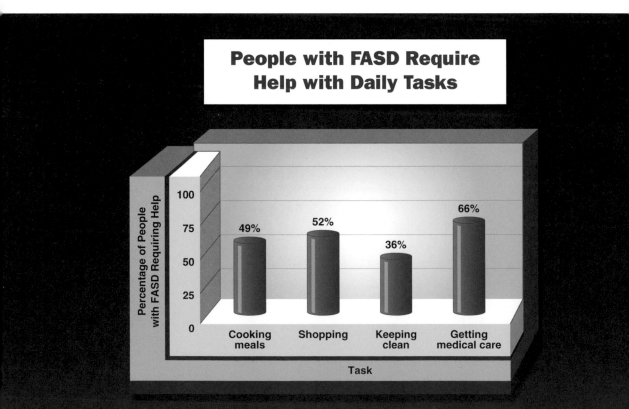

People with FASD Require Help with Daily Tasks

(Percentage of People with FASD Requiring Help, by Task)

- Cooking meals: 49%
- Shopping: 52%
- Keeping clean: 36%
- Getting medical care: 66%

Taken from: Substance Abuse and Mental Health Services Administration, Fetal Alcohol Syndrome Disorders Center for Excellence, "Independent Living for People with Fetal Alcohol Spectrum Disorders." www.fascenter.samhsa.gov.

Her boss, store manager Mary Harrell, says she knew a little about fetal alcohol syndrome before Adams told her she had it. Harrell says she and the other store employees are willing to work around Adam's sometimes inconsistent behavior.

"Probably the area that I see it the most is the disorganization part of it. We just all work with it," says Harrell. "If we have to clean up after her or, you know, pick things up or rearrange things, I'm willing to sacrifice that, because she's just an incredibly talented, creative person and is great with customers. I guess in any job you're going to have people that do certain things better than others."

Adams says she has a short fuse and works hard to keep her emotions in check. One of her biggest challenges is managing money, and trouble with short-term memory makes that even tougher.

Sometimes she forgets to pay bills, though she's gotten better. She says she's lost track of how many times she's had her driver's license suspended for forgetting to pay insurance or renew her license tabs.

"I mean seriously, if I were to rack up collective damages from fines—I'm talking everything from legal system fines to credit card debts to cell phone bills, long distance bills—I'm talking well over $10,000," says Adams.

> **FAST FACT**
>
> According to the Institute of Medicine, the neurobehavioral effects of alcohol on the developing fetus are far more serious than those produced by cocaine, heroin, marijuana, or any other substance of abuse.

"A Wicked Fountain of Youth"

Adams has become an advocate for others with fetal alcohol brain damage. She's on an advisory board for the Minnesota Organization on Fetal Alcohol Syndrome, and speaks to other young women who are struggling to become adults.

Adams says she used to wonder what she might have become had her biological mother not drunk alcohol while she was pregnant. Now, she just focuses on keeping her life together, and accepting the times when that's not possible.

"People say, 'Oh, you seem so normal. You don't act like you have it,'" says Adams, "and then the next month, I can do something that seems so hare-brained stupid, you can't believe I'm capable of doing that."

Health advocates say that, emotionally, people with fetal alcohol damage often function at half their age. Adams says that's true for her. She says she's figured out how to function as an adult, but she knows that part of her will always be a vulnerable little girl.

"I look at it as kind of a wicked fountain of youth," she says. "Nobody ever looks the age that they appear to be. Nobody acts the age that they appear to be. You are forever a child."

For now, Monica's answer is living at home with her folks. But that doesn't work for everyone.

People with Fetal Alcohol Spectrum Disorder Face Difficulties in the U.S. Justice System

Bruce Gage

In the following article Bruce Gage asserts that people with fetal alcohol spectrum disorder (FASD) face many challenges in the U.S. criminal justice system. Gage says the behavioral problems associated with FASD cause large numbers of affected adults to end up in prison. However, Gage notes, the legal system ignores, or worse, exacerbates, the problems faced by people with FASD. He believes more awareness of FASD is needed in the criminal justice community. Gage is chief of psychiatry for the Washington State Department of Corrections.

The growing number of mentally ill in our correctional systems has been well-publicized and is generally well-accepted at this point. It is perhaps lesser known that there are large numbers of persons with various neurological or neurodevelopmental conditions in the correctional system as well. Often unrecognized are

SOURCE: Bruce Gage, "The Growing Problem of Cognitive Disorders in Corrections," *Iceberg*, June 2009. Copyright © 2007, FASIS. Reproduced by permission.

those with common conditions such as fetal alcohol spectrum disorder (FASD) and traumatic brain injury (TBI). These groups share a similar profile in terms of the kinds of problems they have. Moreover, they are preventable problems that are having substantial adverse impacts on both the sufferers and our community.

Fetal Alcohol Syndrome (FAS), the most severe form of FASD, is estimated to occur at a prevalence of 0.5 to 2.0 cases for every thousand births. . . .

Behavioral Problems Often Lead to Crime

In addition to craniofacial abnormalities (which recede to some extent after adolescence), maternal alcohol use can lead to malformation of the brain, learning disabilities, problems with attention, low IQ and various psychiatric disorders, among other issues. But most germane [relevant] for the correctional population are the related behavioral problems. For instance, around 60% of those with FASD have trouble with the law and 40% spend at least some time in confinement (correctional, mental health or drug/alcohol treatment). About 50% engage in repeated sexually inappropriate behavior.

Similarly, traumatic brain injury (including closed head injury not necessarily associated with loss of consciousness) is associated with behavioral problems in addition to a wide array of other difficulties. These disorders typically manifest as impaired executive function giving rise to poor planning, difficulty anticipating outcomes, and, perhaps most importantly, impairment in impulse control and poor social skills. This leads to behaviors that are either themselves criminal or to behaviors such as drug and alcohol use that predispose to criminal acts and further impair executive functioning.

Too often, these behavioral problems stemming from TBI or FASD are attributed to antisocial or other personality disorders or simply to moral turpitude [depravity]. Many of these people get into trouble with the law or in school from a young age. They often come from poor or disadvantaged settings where treatment or other interventions may be minimal, and even the presence of cognitive impairment is frequently unappreciated. Behavioral problems and the fact that academics are often difficult for the cognitively impaired can lead to other psychological problems related to poor self-esteem. People with FASD or TBI, and cognitive disorders in general, may then turn to social roles where they can find acceptance but which are often centered on drug use and/or criminal attitudes.

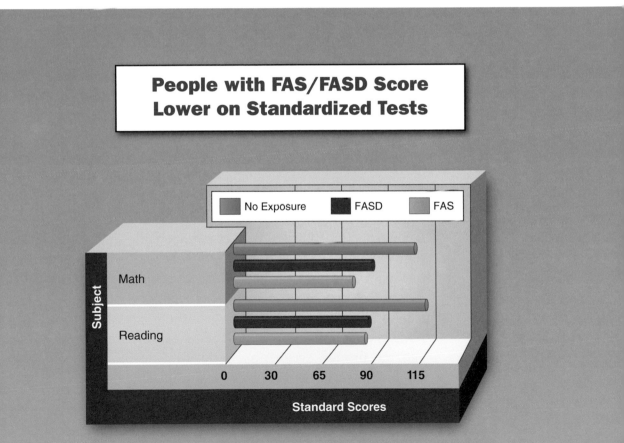

People with FAS/FASD Score Lower on Standardized Tests

Taken from: National Organization on Fetal Alcohol Syndrome, "FASD: What School Systems Should Know About Affected Students," February 16, 2010.

The Justice System and FASD

While those with severe conditions may not be prosecuted because they are too impaired to stand trial, many others do not exhibit obvious cognitive impairment on routine clinical examination, especially when the emphasis is on the detection of serious mental illness rather than cognitive impairments. If those with FASD or TBI are found competent to stand trial, the question of their mental state at the time of the offense may arise. Rarely will these types of disorders lead to an insanity defense as it generally requires a substantial break with reality (psychosis) not typical of these disorders. The degree of *mens rea*, that is the guilty mind or mental state that is an element of most all crimes, might be more relevant but is rarely given proper consideration. A discussion of the legal issues is beyond the scope of this paper, but it can be summarized by noting that problems with executive functioning are rarely considered by the law as long as the person demonstrates some ability to make choices or demonstrate restraint in some circumstances. Mere difficulties with impulse control, even if repetitive, are generally not considered legally relevant.

Because many people who suffer from these sorts of cognitive impairments often have early and frequent behavioral problems, they represent a relatively high risk of re-offense. Rather than their disorders being mitigating, they may be treated as aggravating whether by virtue of the histories alone or, if the impairment does happen to be detected, because of the known associations with behavioral problems. In general, this group of people does not tend to engender sympathy. This is exacerbated by the general, though erroneous, belief that nothing can be done with such neurological conditions, a belief shared by many clinicians. The tendency to therapeutic nihilism [a belief that nothing can be done] becomes a further reason to promote incarceration rather than treatment. And with worsening budgetary pressures on the public mental health system it is likely that the numbers of people with these problems will continue to grow in correctional settings in parallel with those suffering from mental illness.

In this regard, it is important to note that people with FASD or TBI tend to show a limited response to punishment. Given the rapid turnover and limited resources in jails, it is highly unlikely that repeated jailing for minor offenses will yield much change. While the prisons have somewhat more to offer, they are not yet well prepared for working with this population, having their hands already full with a progressively more medically and mentally ill population. Thus, it is unlikely that the current direction of our overall system is heading in a direction that is likely to reduce the frequency of the behavioral problems associated with these disorders.

A mentally ill inmate sits alone in an Idaho prison. Prisons are not equipped to deal with adults who have FAS or other mental disorders. (AP Images)

Making matters worse, these are people with limited advocacy. Coupled with the fact that their behavior is often viewed as blameworthy, it is hard to see where the change is going occur. But many correctional administrators and clinicians are aware of this growing problem and some are undertaking an effort to better detect those with cognitive limitations. This will be a challenge for jails that may not have the time or resources to do the kinds of testing necessary to detect those that are not already identified as cognitively impaired.

Unlike people with serious mental illness or more severe cognitive limitations, who are more readily detected with a clinical interview, those with milder or less obvious cognitive limitations may appear to require no specialized services in the correctional setting. Yet we may believe that they merit more attention for a variety of reasons including the potential for being victimized, their frequent infractions and high recidivism owing to the above-mentioned executive function limitations. They also pose a challenge for correctional rehabilitation and offender programming. Given the frequently associated learning disabilities, more diverse methods are needed than are typically available in correctional settings. Medications hold promise for some and dramatic results, while not the norm, do occur.

TBI is somewhat more frequently diagnosed than FASD, but there are no good studies of the prevalence of these conditions in correctional settings. One group did find that 87% in a jail population had a history of head injury and 29% had moderate to severe head injury. . . . Whatever the actual number of those with TBI or FASD entering the criminal justice system, it is probably comparable in scope to serious mental illness and yet largely silent.

FAST FACT

According to the National Organization on Fetal Alcohol Syndrome, 35 percent of those with FASD over the age of twelve have been incarcerated at some point in their lives.

Awareness of FASD Needed in Justice System

What is encouraging is that the combination of early detection of FASD and being raised in a stable environment can reduce the odds of a bad outcome by 2–4 times. Given that up to 80% of those with FASD do not grow up with their biological mothers, the challenge and the charge is clear. Similarly, aggressive rehabilitation and ongoing services, especially cognitive and behavioral strategies and medication, reduce the negative outcomes in TBI. But most with mild to moderate TBI receive no specialized services despite the well-documented potential for long-term problems. More must be done early in life to secure a better future for those suffering these disorders and for society.

As a clinician going into prisons, it is clear that the problem is substantial. Virtually every day in the prison clinic there is a man or woman presenting for mental health care that has the stigmata [signs] of FASD or clear evidence of TBI, yet few carry the diagnosis. Raising awareness in the community and in corrections is critical if we are to better address their needs—hopefully prior to incarceration.

CHAPTER 2

Controversies Surrounding Fetal Alcohol Syndrome

There Is No Safe Amount of Drinking for Pregnant Women

Fetal Alcohol Spectrum Disorders Study Group

In the following article the Fetal Alcohol Spectrum Disorders Study Group contends that light drinking is harmful to a developing fetus and is not beneficial, as some news reports have suggested. The authors rail against news reports that they say misinterpret the results of a study on the effects of light drinking (defined as having fewer than one or two drinks per week) on unborn children. According to the news reports, children born to mothers who drink lightly during pregnancy may have fewer emotional and behavioral problems than children whose mothers abstain from alcohol during pregnancy. The authors say that the news reports are wrong, that there is no doubt that even light drinking is harmful to fetuses, and that women should completely abstain from alcohol while pregnant. The Fetal Alcohol Spectrum Disorders Study Group is a membership of researchers dedicated to studying fetal alcohol syndrome and devising ways to improve the lives of people suffering from it.

Photo on facing page. Whether pregnant women should drink at all is a controversial topic. (© Bubbles Photolibrary/ Alamy)

We are alarmed by a rash of recent newspaper reports suggesting that light drinking during pregnancy may be beneficial for your unborn child. These misleading and irresponsible reports followed a [October 2008] study by [researcher Yvonne] Kelly and colleagues suggesting that three-year-old children whose mothers drank "lightly" during pregnancy were not at risk for certain behavioral problems. The erroneous interpretation by the lay press about some "beneficial" effects of drinking during pregnancy was NOT part of the study's findings. Indeed, the comments by the press also run counter to research studies indicating that low levels of alcohol can damage a fetus.

Study Results Misinterpreted

The results from the study by Kelly and colleagues must be interpreted with extreme caution for reasons that were overlooked in subsequent news reports. First, the "light drinkers" in this study were more socially and economically advantaged compared to both the heavier drinkers and the women who did not drink during pregnancy. Higher socio-economic status is generally associated with better nutrition, prenatal care and postnatal care-giving environments. The study's authors suggested that any apparent differences in child development between the light drinkers and abstainers may be due to social factors, not drinking.

> **FAST FACT**
>
> According to the American Pregnancy Association, each year in the United States, 757,000 women drink alcohol while pregnant.

Second, the study focused only on children up to three years of age. Generally, the adverse effects of light drinking during pregnancy are subtle and may go undetected in young children. However, other group studies of more moderate or "social" drinking levels during pregnancy have shown an adverse impact on multiple aspects of development through adolescence and young adulthood,

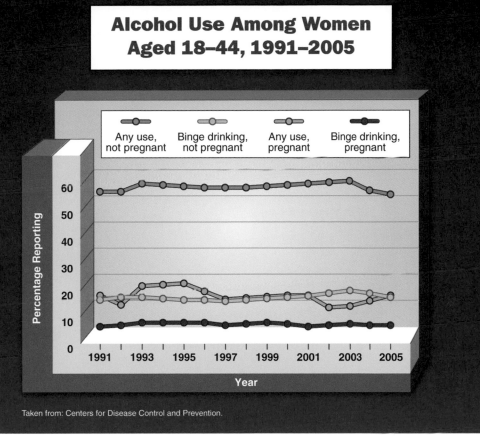

Alcohol Use Among Women Aged 18–44, 1991–2005

Percentage Reporting

Legend:
- Any use, not pregnant
- Binge drinking, not pregnant
- Any use, pregnant
- Binge drinking, pregnant

Year

Taken from: Centers for Disease Control and Prevention.

even when important environmental factors are taken into account.

Third, "light drinking" was defined in the study as anyone who had "no more than one or two drinks a week or no more than two drinks on an occasion." This broad categorization includes patterns of drinking that have been shown to affect fetal brain development in laboratory research studies.

Even Light Drinking Is Harmful

Public health policymakers, health care providers, and the public all want to understand the dangers of alcohol consumption during pregnancy. Studies of pregnant women may not provide clear answers. But carefully controlled laboratory research studies clearly show that the blood alcohol levels that occur with "light drinking" can interfere

Studies have revealed that the adverse effects of light drinking among pregnant women may go undetected in their young children. (James King-Holmes/Photo Researchers, Inc.)

with biological processes that are critical for proper development of the fetal brain. Repeated consumption of this amount of alcohol during pregnancy has also been shown to cause functional brain damage and behavioral problems.

It is an inconvenient fact of life that alcohol is a "teratogen," that is, a chemical that can cause physical or functional birth defects. Prenatal exposure to alcohol is widely accepted to be a risk factor in child development, which may be associated with other prenatal or environmental risk factors. Other risk factors include smoking, stress, poor nutrition and diseases affecting a mother's health, such as diabetes, obesity and high blood pressure. As risk factors accumulate, developmental outcomes are usually less positive.

The consensus recommendation of the hundreds of scientists and clinical investigators, who study Fetal Alcohol Spectrum Disorders, along with public health officials around the world, is very clear—a woman should abstain from drinking during pregnancy as part of an overall program of good prenatal care that includes good nutrition, adequate exercise, sufficient rest, and proper prenatal health care.

Small Amounts of Alcohol Are Probably Safe for Pregnant Women

John C. Hobbins

In the following viewpoint John C. Hobbins asserts that light drinking by a pregnant woman is probably not that harmful to a developing fetus. Hobbins discusses a recent study he conducted in Australia, where attitudes against pregnant women drinking alcohol are not as strong as they are in the United States. Hobbins's results suggest that "low alcohol consumption," defined as fewer than three drinks per week, does not affect fetal growth or increase the risk of premature birth. The results show that smoking is a much bigger contributor to adverse fetal outcomes than is alcohol use. Hobbins says it is likely that large amounts of alcohol are needed to cause full-blown fetal alcohol syndrome. Hobbins is the chief of obstetrics at the University of Colorado Health Sciences Center and associate editor of the *OB/GYN Clinical Alert*.

It has been very difficult to study the effects of alcohol on the fetus and on pregnancy, in general, because one depends so heavily on a patient's candor regarding true alcohol consumption and the effect of confounding variables, such as smoking. In Australia, drinking some alcoholic beverages in pregnancy is quite common, and, as opposed to the United States where drinking even the smallest amount of alcohol is strongly discouraged, the Australian National Health and Medical Research Council in 2001 recommended that "if women choose to drink during pregnancy, they should have less than 7 standard drinks per week and, on any one day, no more than two standard drinks."

Australian Mothers and Alcohol Use

With this backdrop in mind, a group of Australian investigators studied a random sample of 4719 women who delivered [a baby] in Western Australia between 1995 and 1997. The sample represented 10% of births in the region, and information regarding alcohol consumption was obtained via questionnaires sent out after birth. The authors were interested in 2 outcomes: the number of preterm births—defined as those delivering before 37 weeks—and the incidence of small-for-gestational age (SGA) births. To quantify the latter outcome, an optimal birth weight was calculated using the sex of the infant, maternal height, parity, and gestational age. Then the actual birth weight was matched up to this and, if it was below the 10th percentile, the infant was considered to be SGA.

As to alcohol consumption, the authors coded "low" as < 3 drinks per week, "moderate" as 2–5 drinks per week, "heavy" as > 7 drinks per week, and "bingeing" as > 2 drinks at a time (although this was difficult to sort out from the paper). In this random sampling, about 50% did consume some alcohol during pregnancy. Those in the low-level category who continued to drink showed little

Alcohol Use by Pregnant Women Has Increased Slightly Since 2002

Percentage of pregnant women drinking alcohol in the past month:

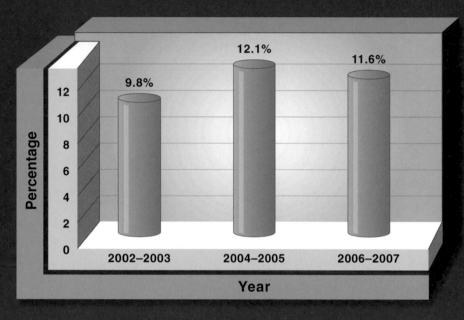

Taken from: National Survey on Drug Use and Health, "Alcohol Use Among Pregnant Women and Recent Mothers: 2002–2007," September 11, 2008.

change in their drinking patterns. However, in all the other categories, there was a general decrease in the average consumption of alcohol. Interestingly, the percentage of heavy and binge drinkers decreased by two-thirds during pregnancy.

The punch line is that in each category there was no statistically significant difference in the rate of preterm birth in any category compared with abstainers. However, if data from the low-level group, representing the largest study

PERSPECTIVES ON DISEASES AND DISORDERS

group, were excluded from the analysis, then there was a 78% increase in preterm births over abstainers. The incidence of SGA was higher among heavy and binge drinkers (13%), compared with the rate in the overall population (8.9%). However, since the heavy and binge group was heavily spiked with smokers, there was no difference in the incidence of SGA when the authors accounted for this confounding variable. The strangest result was that heavy drinkers who stopped drinking before the second trimester had the highest rate of preterm birth.

No Effect on Growth or Prematurity from Light Drinking

In a matter of 40 years, the pendulum has swung from clinicians infusing huge amounts of IV alcohol to stop preterm labor to, now, telling patients that any amount of alcohol consumed by a mother may be dangerous to the health of her fetus. In Europe and, now I realize, in Australia, there is a more relaxed approach to alcohol and pregnancy. The above study does not address the effects of alcohol in small doses on the fetal brain, but it does address two issues—its effect on fetal growth and preterm birth. The bottom line is that, with one exception, there is no major effect on these two outcomes, if the confounding variable of maternal smoking is taken into account.

The surprise finding was that when heavy or binge drinkers stopped drinking after the first trimester, they had the highest rate of preterm birth (13%). The authors postulate that sudden abstinence "may trigger an inflammatory or other metabolic response resulting in an elevation of cytokines" responsible for preterm labor. My guess is that this result could have been due to the small numbers of patients in this category (type 1 error). However, the authors justifiably

> **FAST FACT**
>
> In 2008 the National Survey on Drug Use and Health found that nearly 16 percent of pregnant women aged fifteen to seventeen used alcohol, consuming an average of twenty-four drinks per month.

make the case that if heavy or binge drinkers were to stop or modify this activity before or in early pregnancy, we would not have to worry about this unexpected finding.

Speaking of worry, a few years back we were interested in correlating measurements of certain areas of the fetal brain with alcohol consumption and, then, later, with sophisticated testing of reaction times in the same children. To make a long story short, we found that indirect measurements of the size of the fetal frontal lobe correlated inversely with the amount of alcohol consumed. This, in turn, correlated with how poorly the children performed during the above testing process. However, there was no discernible effect unless the average alcohol consumption exceeded 2.9 drinks per day at the time of entry into the study.

Smoking and alcohol certainly seem to go together, even in pregnant women. For example, the two of us doing the fetal ultrasound measurements in the above study were supposedly blind to which patients were imbibers and which ones were controls, but it became immediately clear who was who, because, often, soon after the "exposed" patients walked in, the ultrasound room smelled like the smoking lounge at Denver International Airport.

Smoking More Harmful than an Occasional Drink

At least one-third of those in the "exposed" group in our study were in the restaurant business where it is common to have "a pop or two" before going home, and most of these individuals stopped after finding out (sometimes late) that they were pregnant. Many of them seemed to exude guilt, fueled by all the warnings out there against any exposure to alcohol. Fortunately, most available data suggest that their guilt is likely unfounded, since it appears at this time that to create full-blown fetal alcohol syndrome, or, it seems, to cause even less severe effects on the fetal brain, larger amounts of alcohol would need to be

Those who say light drinking during pregnancy is acceptable contend that smoking is more harmful during pregnancy than an occasional drink. (© **Bubbles Photolibrary/Alamy**)

consumed regularly. The Australian study indicates that the same could be said for preterm birth and IUGR [intrauterine growth restriction]. Although smaller amounts of consumed alcohol cannot be completely excluded as having subtle effects on the fetal brain, there is much more evidence out there to indicate that smoking is more detrimental to the fetus than an occasional glass of wine.

Women Need to Hear That FAS Is Completely Preventable

Richard H. Carmona

In the following article Richard H. Carmona contends that women need to know that they should abstain from alcohol if they are pregnant or if they are considering becoming pregnant. He says that fetal alcohol syndrome and other alcohol-related birth defects are completely preventable if women do not drink while pregnant. Carmona is concerned because it appears that many pregnant women are continuing to drink and putting their unborn babies at risk. Carmona was the U.S. surgeon general from 2002 until 2006.

Thirty-two years ago [1973], United States researchers first recognized fetal alcohol syndrome (FAS). FAS is characterized by growth deficiencies (or decreased growth), abnormal facial features (specific facial features), and central nervous system (or brain) abnormalities. FAS falls under the spectrum of adverse outcomes caused by prenatal alcohol exposure called Fetal

SOURCE: Richard H. Carmona, "U.S. Surgeon General Releases Advisory on Alcohol Use in Pregnancy," U.S. Department of Health and Human Services, February 21, 2005.

Alcohol Spectrum Disorders (FASD). The discovery of FAS led to considerable public education and awareness initiatives informing women to limit the amount of alcohol they consume while pregnant. But since that time, more has been learned about the effects of alcohol on a fetus. It is now clear that no amount of alcohol can be considered safe.

Importance of Not Drinking Alcohol While Pregnant

I now wish to emphasize to prospective parents, healthcare practitioners, and all childbearing-aged women, especially those who are pregnant, the importance of not

Linda Ohlemiller, director of the St. Louis Arc, a Missouri agency that helps people with developmental disabilities, uses dolls to explain the effects of FAS. The doll on the left displays FAS symptoms. (Karen Elshout/ MCT/Landov)

drinking alcohol if a woman is pregnant or considering becoming pregnant.

Based on the current, best science available we now know the following:

- Alcohol consumed during pregnancy increases the risk of alcohol related birth defects, including growth deficiencies, facial abnormalities, central nervous system impairment, behavioral disorders, and impaired intellectual development.
- No amount of alcohol consumption can be considered safe during pregnancy.
- Alcohol can damage a fetus at any stage of pregnancy. Damage can occur in the earliest weeks of pregnancy, even before a woman knows that she is pregnant.
- The cognitive deficits and behavioral problems resulting from prenatal alcohol exposure are lifelong.
- Alcohol-related birth defects are completely preventable.

For these reasons:

1. A pregnant woman should not drink alcohol during pregnancy.
2. A pregnant woman who has already consumed alcohol during her pregnancy should stop in order to minimize further risk.
3. A woman who is considering becoming pregnant should abstain from alcohol.
4. Recognizing that nearly half of all births in the United States are unplanned, women of child-bearing age should consult their physician and take steps to reduce the possibility of prenatal alcohol exposure.
5. Health professionals should inquire routinely about alcohol consumption by women of childbearing age, inform them of the risks of alcohol consumption during pregnancy, and advise them not to drink alcoholic beverages during pregnancy.

FAS Is Completely Preventable

In the United States, FAS is the leading preventable birth defect with associated mental and behavioral impairment. There are many individuals exposed to prenatal alcohol who, while not exhibiting all of the characteristic features of FAS, do manifest lifelong neurocognitive and behavioral problems arising from this early alcohol exposure. In the United States, the prevalence of FAS is between 0.5 to 2 cases per 1,000 births. It is estimated that for every child born with FAS, three additional children are born who may not have

Alcohol Use by Women of Childbearing Age

Prevalence Estimates of Alcohol Use
Among Women Aged 18 to 44 Years, 2008

WA 53.1 14.8
OR 53.0 12.9
ID 45.0 12.9
MT 54.4 19.3
ND 54.0 23.0
MN 56.9
WY 49.1 15.0
SD 57.0 19.4
NE 53.2 18.9
IA 58.2 22.9
WI 68.4 23.9
MI 58.8 18.7
NY 51.1 12.8
VT 64.0
ME 58.7 18.2
NH 61.2 12.5
MA 63.1 19.5
NV 51.7 10.0
UT 20.4 6.5
CO 56.6 14.7
KS 49.2 12.8
MO 49.2 16.0
IL 55.4 19.4
IN 47.6 12.3
OH 47.6 12.3
PA 52.5 18.9
WV 28.8 8.8
VA 49.5 14.7
RI 56.0 15.1
CT 63.9
CA 43.3 12.8
AZ 51.6 15.5
NM 42.6 10.0
OK 43.6 11.6
AR 39.8 11.1
TN 31.7
KY 9.9 8.0
NC 40.4 11.8
SC 40.8 11
NJ 52.3 14.8
D.C. 62.1 21.3
MD 53.8 14.6
DE 55.2 14.1
MS 35.3 8.9
AL 38.1 9.5
GA 47.1 12.5
TX 40.9 11.3
LA 45.6 10.7
FL 47.7 10.9
Guam 28.6
AK 46.1 12.0
HI 44.7
U.S. Virgin Islands 41.7 6.1
Puerto Rico 25.2 7.3

Any Use

Binge

Taken from: Centers for Disease Control and Prevention.

the physical characteristics of FAS but still experience neurobehavioral deficits resulting from prenatal alcohol exposure that affect learning and behavior.

The outcomes attributable to prenatal alcohol exposure for the children of women whose alcohol consumption averages seven to 14 drinks per week include deficits in growth, behavior, and neurocognition such as problems in arithmetic, language and memory; visual-spatial abilities; attention; and deficits in speed of information processing. Patterns of exposure known to place a fetus at greatest risk include binge drinking, defined as having five or more drinks at one time, and drinking seven or more drinks per week.

> **FAST FACT**
>
> According to the Centers for Disease Control and Prevention, in the United States about 130,000 pregnant women each year drink at levels shown to increase the risk of having a child with FASD.

Despite public health advisories and subsequent efforts to disseminate this information, including a Surgeon General's advisory in 1981, recent data indicate that significant numbers of women continue to drink during pregnancy, many in a high-risk manner that places the fetus at risk for a broad range of problems arising from prenatal alcohol exposure including fetal alcohol syndrome. For example, data suggest that rates of binge drinking and drinking seven or more drinks per week among both pregnant women and non-pregnant women of childbearing age have not declined in recent years. Many women who know they are pregnant report drinking at these levels.

In addition, recent analysis of obstetrical textbooks suggests that physicians may not be receiving adequate instruction in the dangers of prenatal alcohol exposure. The American College of Obstetricians and Gynecologists advises against drinking at all during pregnancy. Nevertheless, only 24 percent of obstetrical textbooks published since 1990 recommended abstinence during pregnancy, despite 30 years of research since the first publications proposed a link between alcohol exposure and birth defects. Scientific evidence amassed in these decades has fortified the rationale for the original advisory against alcohol consumption during pregnancy. Continuing research has generated a wealth of new knowledge on the nature of fetal alcohol-induced injury, the underlying mechanisms of damage, concurrent risk factors, and the clinical distinction of alcohol-related deficits from other disorders.

Saying That FAS Is Completely Preventable Is Misleading

Gideon Koren

In the following viewpoint Gideon Koren contends that the U.S. surgeon general's message that fetal alcohol syndrome is "completely preventable" is off the mark. Koren argues that telling women to be completely abstinent during pregnancy is unrealistic and does not appreciate the varied experiences of women from different walks of life. Koren is a Canadian pediatrician and the founder of the University of Toronto's Motherisk program, which works toward reducing the risks to the fetus from exposure to drugs, alcohol, and other teratogens.

In February 2005 the US Surgeon General released a statement which focused attention on the need to acknowledge Fetal Alcohol Spectrum Disorder (FASD) as a major source of child disability. The statement reiterates key elements of prevention, diagnosis and management of FASD. In it the Surgeon General recites a

SOURCE: Gideon Koren, "February 2005 Surgeon General Statement on Fetal Alcohol Syndrome—A Second Thought," *Journal of Fetal Alcohol Syndrome International*, vol. 3, August 2005. Copyright © The Hospital for Sick Children 2005. Reproduced by permission.

commonly used statement that FASD is "completely preventable." This statement, which appears in hundreds of previous documents, stems from the logic that "if 100% of the etiology [cause] of FASD is maternal drinking, then by prevention of maternal drinking one can prevent 100% of FASD." Stating that "FASD is completely preventable" means then, that alcohol addiction and alcoholism among women of reproductive ages is 100% preventable. Or is it?

Alcoholism among women is a multifactorial, complex and pervasive medical condition. In an era when we have managed to decrease morbidity and mortality of cardiovascular disease, cancer and other serious conditions, there is no evidence for any breakthrough in dealing with the increasing numbers of alcoholic women. Hence, the declaration that FASD is 100% preventable is inaccurate, misleading and can be counter-productive.

As U.S. surgeon general in 2005, Richard Carmona (pictured) released a statement contending that FAS is completely preventable. Some experts disagreed with this conclusion. (AP Images)

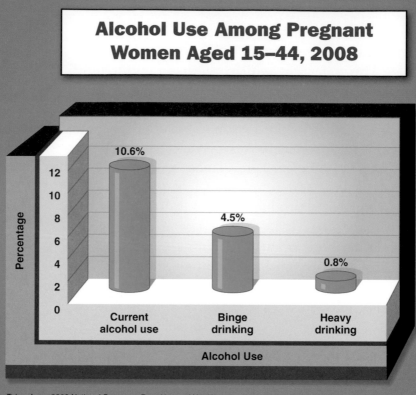

Alcohol Use Among Pregnant Women Aged 15–44, 2008

10.6%

4.5%

0.8%

Percentage

12
10
8
6
4
2
0

Current
alcohol use

Binge
drinking

Heavy
drinking

Alcohol Use

Taken from: 2008 National Survey on Drug Use and Health.

Interestingly, just a few months after the release of the Surgeon General's statement on FASD the new Pope, Benedictus the 16th, declared that the Church's strategy for fighting HIV/AIDS in Africa is still the best, citing celibacy as the only way to eradicate this epidemic.

It is sad when the Surgeon General and the Pope, two of the most influential people in the world when it comes to affecting public health, share the same narrow vision. What is needed is a wider view that acknowledges different patterns of human behavior and experience.

Maybe if we replace "totally preventable" with concepts of "harm reduction" we will develop more realistic end points and achieve them too.

FAS Prevention Should Focus on Stopping Fetal Exposure to Alcohol

Mark B. Mengel, H. Russell Searight, and Keely Cook

In the following viewpoint Mark B. Mengel, H. Russell Searight, and Keely Cook assert that efforts to reduce fetal alcohol syndrome (FAS) should focus on preventing alcohol-exposed pregnancies. The authors contend that family physicians can help reduce FAS by using screening tools and other methods to identify pregnant women who are drinking alcohol and by intervening to prevent further harm to the fetus. Mengel, Searight, and Cook are researchers in the Department of Community and Family Medicine at St. Louis University in St. Louis, Missouri.

Effects of alcohol on the developing fetus are multifocal, incurable, pernicious, and extremely costly; however, these effects are eminently preventable. Despite the federal government warning that drinking alcohol during pregnancy is unsafe, and the fact that a safe

SOURCE: Mark B. Mengel, H. Russell Searight, and Keely Cook, "Preventing Alcohol-Exposed Pregnancies," *Journal of the American Board of Family Medicine*, vol. 19, September/October 2006, pp. 494–495, 501–502. Copyright © 2006 by the American Board of Family Medicine. Reproduced by permission.

threshold for alcohol consumption during pregnancy has not been demonstrated to exist either in human or animal studies, a substantial proportion of women self-report that they continue to drink during pregnancy. Due to the continued high prevalence of drinking alcohol during pregnancy, the US Department of Health and Human Services has established a Healthy People 2010 goal to increase the number of pregnant women who report abstinence from alcohol use during the past month from a baseline rate in 1996 to 1997 of 86% to a 2010 target of 94%. In 2004, the US Preventive Services Task Forces recommended screening and counseling intervention in primary care settings to reduce alcohol misuse in adults, including pregnant women.

Defining Alcohol-Exposed Pregnancy

Given the emphasis on prevention of adverse alcohol effects in the fetus through abstinence or drinking reduction in the mother, the term alcohol-exposed pregnancy (AEP) has been coined to help clinicians judge exposure status. AEP is defined as any pregnancy during which a woman drank any amount of alcohol at any time during her pregnancy. All fertile, sexually active, childbearing-aged women are at risk for an AEP if they drink alcohol, are sexually active, and do not use contraception effectively. Preventing an AEP can be accomplished through 2 mechanisms: 1) engaging in abstinence from alcohol use before and during pregnancy, or 2) preventing pregnancy entirely by engaging in effective methods of contraception or abstaining from sexual activity.

Family physicians can play a significant role in preventing AEP. Family physicians provide a significant portion of the primary care to childbearing-aged women in this country, and many family physicians continue to care

FAST FACT

Binge drinking for a woman is defined as having four or more drinks on one occasion.

Obstetrician-Gynecologists' Concerns About Preconception Care

When meeting with women who plan to become pregnant, obstetricians and gynecologists typically discuss four issues of critical importance in ensuring the health of both mother and fetus. The ranking of these issues by physicians, in order of importance, appears below.

Rank	Issue
1	Cigarette smoking
2	Folic acid supplements
3	Illegal drug use
4	Alcohol consumption

Taken from: Maria Morgan, Debra Hawks, and Stanley Zinberg, "What Obstetrician-Gynecologists Think of Preconception Care," *Maternal and Child Health Journal*, September 2006.

for pregnant women. Prevention is recognized as one of the core tenets of family medicine, and family medicine physicians are generally among the best trained primary care physicians in dealing with issues of substance abuse and mental health. In surveys, many family physicians believe that dealing with substance use and abuse issues is within their purview as primary care physicians. By working to prevent AEP, family physicians can play a significant role in preventing the adverse effects of alcohol exposure on the developing fetus. . . .

Physicians Can Help Prevent Alcohol-Exposed Pregnancies

Current evidence suggests that if family medicine physicians engage in routine screening, assessment, education, and intervention in women of childbearing age regarding their use of alcohol that the risk of AEP will be decreased.

Family physicians can provide education, routine screening and assessment, and, if necessary, intervention to address their patients' use of alcohol. (© Judy Collins/Alamy)

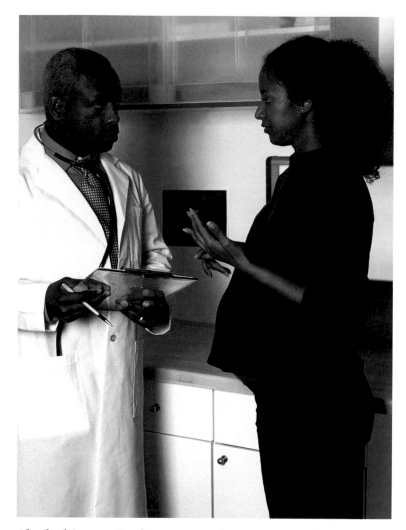

Alcohol is a toxin that can result in a range of abnormalities in children; perhaps, the most devastating of which are the neurobehavioral and central nervous system effects. Although profoundly disturbing in their on way, these initial neurobehavioral and cognitive affects result in secondary disabilities in the teenage years that often preclude these individuals from reaching independence as adults. Because these FASD do not occur in the absence of prenatal alcohol exposure and because there is no known cure once they have occurred, preventing an AEP is the most logical intervention strategy for this problem at this time.

Integrating these intervention techniques within family medicine practice will not be easy. Current research suggests that the involvement of the staff and the design of effective office systems could take most of the burden of performing these activities off the family physician and might be the most effective way of integrating these practices within family practice.

Clearly further translational research is needed to determine the best ways to integrate these practices within the busy family medicine office setting. Practice-based research networks would be an ideal laboratory for carrying out this translational research. Such research should focus on the effectiveness of these practices in the family medicine office setting and determine their impact on reducing alcohol-exposed pregnancy risk and decreasing the prevalence of FASD.

FAS Prevention Should Focus on Helping Alcohol-Abusing Women

Janet Golden

In the following viewpoint Janet Golden says that providing treatment to alcohol-abusing women is the best way to prevent fetal alcohol syndrome (FAS). Golden details the history of FAS and says that the needs of alcohol-abusing women have gotten short shrift in all the talk of preventing FAS. Helping alcohol-abusing women to stop drinking would prevent the birth of many FAS babies, the author contends. Golden is a historian and the author of the 2005 book *Message in a Bottle: The Making of Fetal Alcohol Syndrome*.

If you've ever cringed while watching a pregnant woman take a drink, perhaps it is because you've seen the warning labels on bottles of alcohol or read Michael Dorris' book, *The Broken Cord,* about his son's struggles with fetal alcohol syndrome [FAS]. Maybe you've seen a public service announcement, a high school science textbook or a magazine article about FAS.

SOURCE: Janet Golden, "Stopping Fetal Alcohol Syndrome: Women Who Drink Need Treatment," *Seattle Post-Intelligencer*, March 20, 2005. Reproduced by permission of the author.

Perhaps you keep up with the news and know that [in February 2005], the U.S. Surgeon General updated a 1981 warning advising pregnant women and those who might become pregnant to abstain from drinking in order to prevent the birth defects caused by prenatal alcohol exposure. Absent from this warning was a call for increased services (including insurance coverage for treatment) for alcohol-abusing women.

The most serious effect of prenatal alcohol exposure is fetal alcohol syndrome. People with FAS often have problems with learning, memory, attention span, communication, vision and hearing. They struggle with difficulties in school and have problems getting along with others. Thousands are born with the condition each year, adding to an already large population of FAS-damaged individuals.

History of FAS

The modern history of FAS began in Seattle in 1973 when medical researchers at the University of Washington reported that alcohol was a teratogen, an agent that causes birth defects. The announcement was greeted with understandable skepticism. If alcohol exposure in utero harmed fetuses, why had no one noticed before? Alcohol, critics correctly pointed out, had a long history of use and abuse.

In fact, credible medical reports about the effects of alcohol on fetuses had been appearing for a century—but to little notice. Physicians and the public paid attention in 1973 because they had learned, dramatically, that the womb was not a barrier protecting the fetus. Revelations in the 1960s about birth defects caused by thalidomide [an anti-nausea drug] and by a rubella epidemic quickly educated the public about fetal health.

Subsequently, the women's health movement brought women's alcoholism out of the shadows with demands for new research and treatment protocols. With these changes

In the 1960s the connection between birth defects and use by pregnant women of the drug thalidomide—which caused birth defects in children—first raised public awareness about fetal health. (**AP Images**)

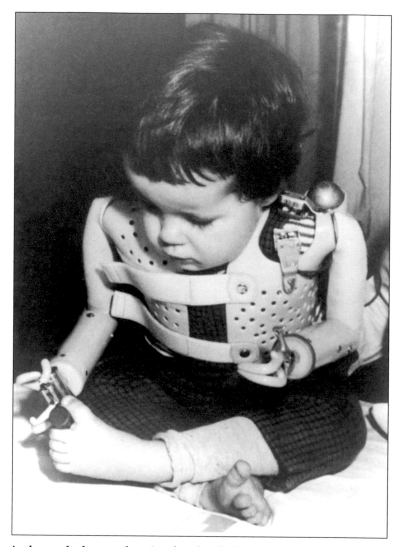

in knowledge and attitude, the federal government sponsored studies and issued a warning.

In 1977 the National Institute on Alcohol Abuse and Alcoholism declared that when pregnant women consumed six or more drinks a day, they significantly raise their risk of bearing a child with birth defects. By 1981 the warning broadened when the acting Surgeon General cautioned pregnant women and those thinking of becoming pregnant "not to drink alcoholic beverages."

A number of cities and states promptly took action to prevent FAS, mandating that warnings appear in places where alcoholic beverages were sold. Then, in 1988, Congress passed legislation calling for warnings on alcoholic beverages. The labels, warnings and cautionary publicity proved effective in reaching millions of women who subsequently chose to abstain from drinking during pregnancy. Others, especially those with severe drinking problems, often failed to heed the warnings. Rates of FAS did not decline.

Shortly before the bottle labels appeared, America's only "failure to warn" case against an alcoholic beverage manufacturer began in Seattle. The issue in *Thorp v. Jim Beam* revolved around the questions of whether Michael Thorp had FAS and, if so, whether the company should be held responsible.

Discussions of the trial reflected larger cultural questions. Were alcoholic beverage manufacturers to blame when their products were misused? Did manufacturers have a duty to warn against misuse? Were pregnant women alone responsible for the health of their fetuses or did society have a responsibility as well? In this case, the jury found in favor of the distilling company, but the questions raised during the trial continued to be debated.

A few years after the Seattle trial, public concern about crack cocaine brought new attention to the problem of substance abuse by pregnant women. Media attention to crack-using pregnant women unfortunately moved accounts of FAS from public health reporting to crime news.

Vilifying Pregnant Women and FAS

Demonization of substance-abusing women did little to prevent problems or help babies. In some places women faced arrest for giving birth to babies showing signs of drug or alcohol exposure. Elsewhere, there were calls to put addicted women into preventive detention during pregnancy.

Policing of alcohol-abusing pregnant women never occurred to the same extent as it did with women using illegal drugs. It was, however, part of the same impulse. Clamor about "personal" responsibility drowned out public health and substance abuse experts who demanded, in the name of "social" responsibility, more services and care for women in the grip of addiction.

As women giving birth to children with FAS became vilified, so were many teenagers and adults who had been born with the syndrome and were getting into trouble as a result of their cognitive disabilities. Yet, courtroom claims of diminished capacity and postsentencing appeals for clemency based on a diagnosis of FAS sparked a harsh reaction.

Some commentators called FAS an "abuse excuse," denying the legitimacy of the diagnosis. A potent example was the failed 1992 clemency plea of convicted double-murderer Robert Alton Harris, who had an IQ of 67. His death row appeal based on his FAS galvanized the media and the public. Opponents argued that his claim made a mockery of the justice system.

FAST FACT

According to the 2008 National Survey on Drug Use and Health, 8 percent of pregnant women engaged in an episode of binge drinking during their first trimester of pregnancy.

Losing Sight of Alcohol-Abusing Women

In the uproar over the meaning of FAS, the public lost sight of the alcohol-abusing women whose own lives were often cut short by their addiction. Studies of women giving birth to alcohol-affected babies revealed again and again their shockingly high death rates.

In addition to their excess mortality these women, like other alcohol abusers, suffered from terrible physical and psychological disorders linked to their drinking. Yet, their deaths and suffering went largely unnoticed.

Ideas about prevention remained rooted in easy fixes such as warning labels, rather than on the harder, costlier, more necessary and more challenging task of helping women with alcohol problems overcome their addiction. Women faced numerous barriers to treatment, such as the need for child care, the cost of treatment, the opposition of family members and, of course, their denial of their alcoholism.

Such barriers raise a host of questions. How can women be provided with inpatient substance abuse treatment that does not threaten them with the loss of their children? Can we offer parity with other illnesses for health care coverage for substance abuse and mental health? Can we offer universal access to health care that would permit effective diagnosis and intervention in the case of substance abuse problems?

To give some examples of the problems we face, Washington state requires insurance companies to offer chemical dependency benefits to their larger purchasers but

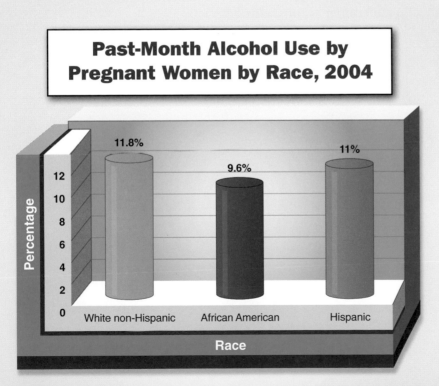

Taken from: Substance Abuse and Mental Health Services Administration, Fetal Alcohol Spectrum Disorders Center for Excellence, "Independent Living for People with Fetal Alcohol Spectrum." www.fascenter.samhsa.gov.

does not require a specific level of coverage. Similarly, Washington's Medicaid program has limited coverage for chemical dependency treatment.

Alcohol-Abusing Women Need Treatment

Over the past 30 or so years, FAS has had many meanings: a medical discovery, a public health problem, a matter of political discussion, a media phenomenon, a morality tale about motherhood and a legal claim. Its medical definition has grown more precise as scientific research has helped to elucidate precisely how alcohol affects the developing brain.

It is time to develop a new social definition. FAS is a birth defect and, equally important, it is an indication that alcohol-abusing women are not getting the help they need. These women don't need warnings, they need treatment. If we provide it, we can prevent their deaths and the births of babies with FAS.

Civil Commitment Laws for Pregnant Drinkers Are Designed to Protect Fetuses

Alcohol Policy Information System

In the following viewpoint the Alcohol Policy Information System (APIS) asserts that state laws that involuntarily commit pregnant women to treatment programs are sometimes necessary to protect unborn children. According to APIS, five states—Minnesota, North Dakota, Oklahoma, South Dakota, and Wisconsin—have these types of civil commitment laws. The Alcohol Policy Information System is a project of the National Institute on Alcohol Abuse and Alcoholism, part of the National Institutes of Health.

Scientific research has established that alcohol consumption during pregnancy is associated with adverse health consequences. Fetal Alcohol Spectrum Disorders (FASD) is the term used to describe the range of birth defects caused by maternal alcohol consumption during pregnancy. FASD are considered the most common nonhereditary cause of mental retardation. Included

SOURCE: *Alcohol Policy Information System: A Project of the National Institute on Alcohol Abuse and Alcoholism.* Bethesda, MD: National Institute on Alcohol Abuse and Alcoholism, 2009.

in Fetal Alcohol Spectrum Disorders is the diagnosis often referred to as Fetal Alcohol Syndrome (FAS), which is the most severe form of FASD. It is characterized by facial defects, growth deficiencies, and central nervous system dysfunction. Also included in FASD are other types of alcohol-induced mental impairments that are just as serious, if not more so, than in children with FAS. The term "alcohol-related neurodevelopmental disorder" (ARND) has been developed to describe such impairments. Prenatally exposed children can also have other alcohol-related physical abnormalities of the skeleton and certain organ systems; these are known as alcohol-related birth defects (ARBD).

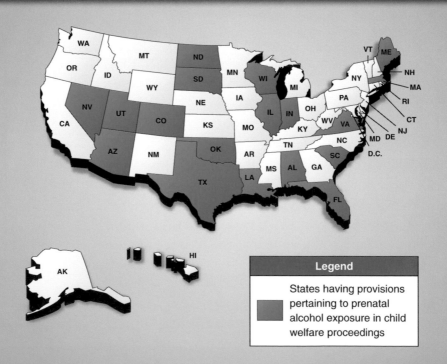

Alcohol and Pregnancy: Legal Significance for Child Abuse/Child Neglect as of January 1, 2009

Legend

States having provisions pertaining to prenatal alcohol exposure in child welfare proceedings

Taken from: National Institute on Alcohol Abuse and Alcoholism, National Institutes of Health, Department of Health and Human Services.

State and Federal governments have established various policies in response to the risks associated with drinking during pregnancy. This section of APIS [Alcohol Policy Information System] addresses involuntary civil commitment of pregnant alcohol abusers. Civil commitment refers either to involuntary commitment of a pregnant woman to treatment or involuntary placement of a pregnant woman in protective custody of the State for the protection of a fetus from prenatal exposure to alcohol. As of January 1, 2008, five jurisdictions have statutory authorization for the civil commitment of women who abuse alcohol during pregnancy: Minnesota, North Dakota, Oklahoma, South Dakota, and Wisconsin.

Two Types of Civil Commitment

There are two types of civil commitments: emergency and judicial. Emergency commitments are short in duration and may be imposed by the administrator of an appropriate mental health facility. Emergency commitment laws are not included in this research or in the coding of this policy topic except as described in this policy description. Judicial commitments are typically lengthier and must be ordered by a court.

The involuntary civil commitment arrangements in North Dakota, Oklahoma, and South Dakota provide for committing pregnant alcohol abusers to treatment facilities. The procedures in those three States are similar. . . .

Minnesota provides two types of civil commitment procedures: early intervention and judicial commitment. Early intervention is of shorter duration and involves a less intrusive program than the standard judicial commitment procedure.

Wisconsin's child welfare laws provide for involuntary civil commitment to a variety of placements including a

> **FAST FACT**
>
> According to the Centers for Disease Control and Prevention, of pregnant women reporting alcohol use from 1991 to 2005, about 18 percent were over the age of thirty-five and 14.4 percent were college graduates.

In 1997 Deborah Zimmerman (pictured) became the first woman in the United States to be charged with harming her fetus due to alcohol abuse. (AP Images)

treatment facility, jail, and a relative's home. In Wisconsin there are three stages leading to a judicial commitment. In the first stage, a woman is taken into protective custody, usually by law enforcement or child protective services. In the second stage, in cases in which there is a substantial health risk to the fetus, the woman may be held (detained) in protective custody for up to 48 hours. In the third stage, if custody is sought for a sustained period of time (i.e., a period longer than provided for in the second stage), the woman is entitled to legal representation and a hearing at which a court determines whether it will enter an order for her continued custody.

Despite their differences, all of these commitment and custody provisions are designed to protect the fetus via the involuntary restriction of the pregnant woman's action or conduct.

Civil Commitment Laws for Pregnant Drinkers Are Problematic

Erin N. Linder

In the following viewpoint Erin N. Linder contends that state laws that punish women for prenatal alcohol abuse are problematic because among other things, they subordinate a woman's rights to that of her fetus. Linder says states such as Wisconsin that commit alcohol-abusing pregnant women for involuntary treatment violate the Constitution, are not practical, and lead states down a slippery slope. Instead of punishing pregnant women for drinking, the author maintains, states should educate them and provide treatment. Linder is an attorney in Illinois.

A lthough American citizens are entitled to certain basic freedoms, new laws aimed at protecting unborn children from the effects of alcohol threaten to rob pregnant women of their fundamental rights. The fetus, on

SOURCE: Erin N. Linder, "Punishing Prenatal Alcohol Abuse: The Problems Inherent in Utilizing Civil Commitment to Address Addiction," *University of Illinois Law Review*, September 21, 2005, pp. 873–75, 881–82, 85, 887–88, 894–96, 899. Copyright © 2005 the Board of Trustees of the University of Illinois, College of Law. Reproduced by permission.

the other hand, is increasingly protected as an independent legal entity, often with interests adverse to a pregnant woman's autonomy. Over the past few decades, legislatures have advanced the idea of a fetal rights doctrine that would permit states to intervene in the maternal-fetal relationship to protect potential human life. Provoked by the crack-cocaine epidemic of the 1980s, states originally focused on prosecuting women who abused illegal drugs during pregnancy for the subsequent harm to their unborn children. Fetal protectionism has gone so far, however, that pregnant women are now being punished for legal behavior that may injure a fetus. . . .

While a fetus traditionally had no rights under the common law, in recent years, states have expanded their role in protecting potential human life. Protections now range from fetal homicide statutes to prosecution of pregnant women for prenatal drug abuse. Some states have gone so far as to enact legislation allowing government officials to take protective custody of pregnant women who abuse alcohol. This type of fetal rights legislation raises a number of questions as to how far a state can intervene to protect fetal health before impermissibly infringing on the sovereignty of pregnant women. . . .

States Are Going Too Far

Although the majority of fetal rights legislation has focused on prenatal drug abuse, a wide spectrum of other behaviors can negatively affect fetal health. Even legal activities such as smoking cigarettes, taking over-the-counter medications, and exercising may impact the well-being of a fetus. The consumption of alcohol is one such activity which has a profound effect on fetal health. In fact, maternal alcohol consumption is considered even more dangerous than prenatal drug abuse because it is more prevalent in society and the leading cause of non-hereditary mental retardation.

Several states, including South Dakota and Wisconsin, have passed criminal legislation directed at pregnant women who consume alcoholic beverages. Wisconsin's civil commitment laws, in particular, have sparked a great deal of controversy. These laws allow the state to take an expectant mother into custody if a public officer finds that she exhibits a "habitual lack of self-control in the use of alcohol beverages." Wisconsin's statutory scheme is a far more draconian approach to protecting fetal rights than previous legislation targeting the use of illegal substances. . . .

After the Wisconsin Supreme Court reversed several cases holding pregnant women liable for harming their fetuses through drug and alcohol use, the Wisconsin legislature responded by revising its Children's Code to create a

After the Wisconsin Supreme Court (pictured) reversed several cases in which pregnant women who abused alcohol had been held criminally responsible for harming their unborn children, the state's legislature revised its Children's Code to create new categories for "unborn child" abuse. (AP Images)

new category of "unborn child" abuse. Wisconsin law places "unborn children" under the jurisdiction of juvenile courts. Accordingly, the state is authorized to take custody of an expectant mother who uses drugs or alcohol during pregnancy and order involuntary inpatient care. . . .

Problems Inherent in State Fetal Protection Laws

Any regulation that punishes or restricts a pregnant woman's behavior in order to protect an unborn fetus essentially subordinates the civil liberties of the woman to the rights of her fetus. This maternal-fetal conflict is especially severe when states attempt to regulate prenatal behavior that is otherwise legal, such as alcohol consumption. Civil commitment schemes which regulate prenatal alcohol consumption, such as Wisconsin's protective custody statute, pose a number of constitutional and practical problems.

First, prenatal alcohol abuse protections may violate both the Due Process and Equal Protection Clauses of the Constitution. Even if these protections pass constitutional scrutiny, they may still be rendered unworkable by the range of practical problems they face. A purely punitive approach to preventing FAS, which forces pregnant women into involuntary treatment, does not address the addiction at hand but, instead, may deter women from seeking proper prenatal care. In addition, proscribing otherwise legal behavior is the first step toward regulating any maternal conduct that may adversely affect the health of a fetus. Further, statutes that simply react to the problem of prenatal alcohol abuse by taking already pregnant women into custody are unlikely to prevent FAS since the fetus has most likely already suffered irreversible damage. . . .

While preventing FAS is a legitimate state objective, civil commitment provisions like Wisconsin's statute do not merely regulate behavior based on the biological ability to procreate. These statutes only punish women, not men, for harming a fetus. Studies show, however, that the biological father's behavior before and even during pregnancy, such as heavy consumption of alcohol before conception, may also have a negative impact on fetal health. . . .

Race discrimination is also important to consider when analyzing the constitutionality of fetal abuse legislation, as the majority of state intervention on the behalf of fetuses is directed at minority women of low socioeconomic standing. Commentators argue that this unequal impact is a result of legislation that "unfairly target[s] minority women as fetal abusers." For instance, state intervention is more likely where the substance at issue is cocaine, which is more likely to be used by minority women. In addition, studies have shown that while minority women are not more likely to use drugs than other groups, they are more likely to

> **FAST FACT**
>
> According to the U.S. Substance Abuse and Mental Health Administration, FAS costs the United States nearly $4 billion each year.

be tested for substance abuse during pregnancy. In fact, one study found that prenatal substance abuse by African American women is almost ten times as likely to be reported to government authorities [as] similar abuse by white women. This discrepancy may be a result of the fact that public hospitals, which often cater to individuals of low-socioeconomic status, are more likely to test and report prenatal substance abuse than private facilities. . . .

In addition to the constitutional problems facing prenatal alcohol abuse statutes, there are also a number of practical issues that make such an approach imprudent. First, punitive measures may deter substance abusing women from seeking prenatal care. Second, a civil commitment approach to preventing FAS fails to address a pregnant woman's alcohol addiction until the most pervasive damage to the fetus has already occurred. Third, civil commitment has a drastic impact on the families of women taken into custody. Finally, prohibiting prenatal alcohol consumption may be the first step toward regulating all behavior that adversely affects a fetus. . . .

Slippery Slope

Wisconsin's civil commitment statute also raises the question of how far a state can intervene in the maternal-fetal relationship. If Wisconsin can civilly commit a pregnant woman for consuming alcohol, it is conceivable that states could similarly impose liability for other legal activities that may result in harm to a fetus, including smoking cigarettes,

**Alcohol and Pregnancy:
Civil Commitment Laws as of January 1, 2009**

Legend

Civil commitment laws related to alcohol and pregnancy

No civil commitment laws related to alcohol and pregnancy

Taken from: Alcohol Policy Information System, National Institute on Alcohol Abuse and Alcoholism, September 28, 2009.

maintaining an unhealthy diet, ignoring physician's instructions, or participating in dangerous sports. For example, a woman in Utah was recently charged with criminal homicide when one of her twins was stillborn after she allegedly refused to undergo a caesarean section that may have saved the unborn child's life. Prosecutors claim the woman's refusal to heed her physician's medical advice and her alleged drug use during pregnancy will factor into the murder case. This case is another example of the growing trend toward protecting the health of a fetus at the expense of the mother. On the whole, allowing states to punish pregnant women for legal behavior that is harmful to a fetus sets a dangerous precedent that could lead to the abrogation [annulment] of women's self-sovereignty.

Focus on Education and Treatment

While a punitive approach to preventing prenatal alcohol abuse may reduce some of the effects of FAS, its benefits are outweighed by a myriad of constitutional and practical problems. Accordingly, states should embrace fetal protection policies which aim to eliminate the long-term problem of alcohol addiction by focusing on education and treatment. Although FAS is a prevalent problem with devastating effects, it is not unpreventable. Simply put, abstinence from alcohol during pregnancy eliminates any risk of alcohol-related birth defects. As such, the key to preventing FAS is early intervention to provide community education, to identify the women who are likely to engage in harmful prenatal behavior, and to provide voluntary substance abuse treatment that promotes a healthy family environment.

CHAPTER 3

Personal Experiences with Fetal Alcohol Syndrome

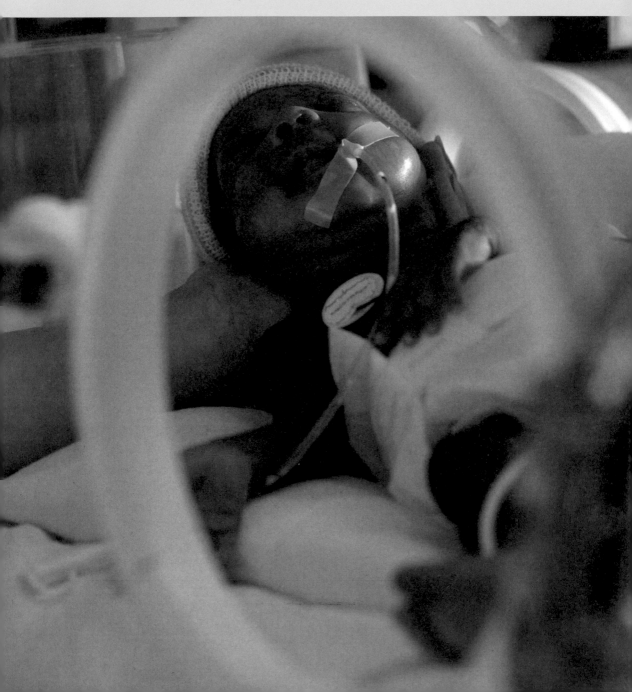

A Regretful Mother

Lorrie Hundal and Marcie Good

In the following article, Lorrie Hundal shares the heartbreak she endures with the knowledge that her use of alcohol while she was pregnant has irreparably hurt her son. Hundal describes to reporter Marcie Good the daily difficulties her son Zach, diagnosed with fetal alcohol spectrum disorder (FASD) at the age of twelve, has faced throughout his life. Hundal shares her heart-rending story in hopes that it will make other pregnant women decide to stop drinking. Hundal lives in British Columbia, Canada.

I t's not easy to admit that I hurt my son. I've stood in front of audiences of more than 900 people and groups as small as eight and told them my story about how drinking alcohol during my pregnancy has affected Zach's life. Reliving the most painful memories of the past 23 years takes every bit of my strength. But it's worth the effort. I know of at least one pregnant woman who heard our story and decided to stop drinking.

I never met her, but I imagine she is young and dealing with her own troubles—just like I was. Back in 1979,

SOURCE: Lorrie Hundal as told to Marcie Good, "A Mom's Fetal Alcohol Syndrome Story: The Obstacles of a Single-Parent Family Coping with an Alcohol-Related Birth Defect," *Canadian Living*, April 2007. Copyright © 2007 Canadian Living. Reproduced by permission.

Photo on facing page. This prematurely born infant suffers from Fetal Alcohol Syndrome. (© **PhotoTake, Inc./Alamy**)

I was 18, had moved out of my parents' home in Coquitlam, B.C. [British Columbia] and had quit school to work. At 23, after a brief affair, I got pregnant. I was excited about the baby but continued drinking and partying with my friends. I didn't think about the consequences.

My life changed after my son was born. I had nothing more to do with the bar scene; Zach was my priority.

When Zach was a baby, I started wondering if something was wrong with him. He didn't reach the same milestones as other children. He rolled instead of crawled, was uncoordinated when he tried to walk, and by age three his speech was so garbled I couldn't understand anything he said. On top of these struggles, he suffered from various allergies. When he was six months old his asthma was so bad that I had to take him to emergency. The doctors tied down his little arms and legs, and put an intravenous tube into the top of his head and an oxygen tent over his body. I stood by and watched him in distress, unable to help him.

Growing Up with FAS

Soon after Zach was born, I went back to school and got my high school equivalency, then went on to college and completed a community social service worker program. I was determined to make a good life for us and to be a positive role model for my son. I got a job as a financial worker for the Ministry of Human Resources.

Zach's difficulties continued. In kindergarten he was suspended for two weeks because of his disruptive behaviour. When he played outside with other kids, I would stand at the door and listen for a squabble. Zach's social skills were delayed, and he often had trouble fitting in. He did not get invited to many birthday parties. I wondered if his future would include a girlfriend, wife, children or a job. I had no idea what I could hope for.

By age eight, he was already seeing a psychiatrist and taking antidepressants. His mental and physical health reached a crisis point when he threatened to run in front of cars. He was committed to the psychiatric unit of a children's hospital, where he stayed for seven weeks. I had recently been diagnosed with multiple sclerosis (MS), and I suffered chronic facial pain and was frequently exhausted. I was working full time and driving two hours from my office to the hospital to see Zach as often as I could. On days when I couldn't manage, I made sure a family member was there. Still, I felt so awful when I missed a day.

I was always honest with Zach's doctors and teachers about my alcohol use during my pregnancy, but I didn't want Zach to carry the stigma of a label. When he was 12 his teachers told me there would be more funding for his support if he was diagnosed, so I took him to a specialist. He determined that Zach did, indeed, have fetal alcohol effects, which falls within fetal alcohol spectrum disorder....

Daily Obstacles

Children like Zach face huge obstacles on a daily basis. Throughout school, he was teased a lot and had low self-esteem. When he was angry he would leave home and not come back, sometimes staying on the street. It got worse after high school. He was depressed and suicidal, and he would even direct his anger at me. He once threatened to damage my car with a screwdriver.

Like many children affected by fetal alcohol syndrome, he has trouble seeing the consequences of his actions when he lashes out. And he's often remorseful. After one blowup we sat together on his bed crying. "You know, Mom," he said. "I don't do that on purpose."

But despite all of Zach's challenges, he always showed a big heart. When I was in pain from MS, he would rub my back for half an hour. Sometimes when I felt ice cold, he would take my blanket and warm it up in the dryer. Even

> **FAST FACT**
>
> According to the U.S. Substance Abuse and Mental Health Administration, the majority of drinkers underestimate the number of fluid ounces they are consuming by about 30 percent.

when he found out that his own problems stemmed from my reckless behaviour, he didn't turn on me. I told him how sorry I was and that if I had a chance to do things over I would. I was sobbing. "Don't feel guilty, Mom," he said. "You were young. I forgive you." His generosity overwhelms me.

Living a Full Life with FAS

He has also had successes. I was so proud when he received two awards in high school, one for culinary arts and one for citizenship. These were presented by staff who saw his progress in developing relationships and wanted to acknowledge his accomplishments. At 18 he got his driver's licence; he is an excellent driver.

Today Zach lives on his own and works as a part-time supervisor at a fast-food restaurant. Holding this position is an incredible achievement for him. He is responsible with money, although it is stressful for him to manage his tight budget. When I visited him recently at his bachelor apartment, he was just coming back from driving a neighbour to the pharmacy to pick up a prescription. He often helps out neighbours, by driving them to appointments or to the store.

I wish he didn't have constant challenges to face every day. He takes more time than others to complete tasks and has problems with coordination. He often feels disheartened about what he sees as an unpromising future.

I help Zach out in as many little ways as I can, such as sending him care packages and giving him financial advice. But how can I not feel guilty when I know my son lives with heartache? The hardest part is knowing that I can't turn back the clock and give him the life he deserves.

Even with my diagnosis of MS, I feel compelled to speak as a mom to try to prevent other women who are pregnant from drinking alcohol. I've spoken at conferences, to youth teams from the local treatment centre and to parent groups. Sharing my story is emotionally draining, but it's worth every minute.

Adopting a Child with FAS

Eva Carner

In the following article Eva Carner recounts the experiences of adopting her son Rick at the age of four and the struggles they both faced in dealing with his fetal alcohol syndrome (FAS). During a crisis when Rick was thirteen years old, Carner said she found a book about FAS that changed her life. From that point on she decided to do everything she could to help prevent other children from being born with FAS. Carner is the project coordinator of the Fetal Alcohol Spectrum Teaching and Awareness Campaign at the Arc Riverside, a Southern California organization committed to improving the lives of people with mental retardation and developmental disabilities.

In 1982, I became the foster mom to Rick, a small child who got a pretty rough start to life and an even rougher "pre" start.

Rick's birth mother was addicted to alcohol and for most of his time in her womb she drank heavily. I was a

SOURCE: Eva Carner, "Eva & Rick's Incredible Journey," *Exceptional Parent*, November 2006, pp. 63–66. Copyright © 2006 EP Global Communications, Inc. Reproduced by permission.

single, special education teacher and worked with children with developmental disabilities for the Riverside County [California] Office of Education. When Rick came to me at the age of 4, I had little knowledge of his special needs and what it would mean to his future, and to mine.

Abuse and Neglect

He wore out his welcome in a few months wherever he went and had survived at least 13 homes by the time he came to live with me. One of his "homes" was the psychiatric ward of a county hospital where he stayed for three months when he was two. Immediately preceding this, he visited his birth mom and returned in a catatonic state. He wouldn't stop rocking and staring into space. His foster parents couldn't break his trance and after a few hours took him to the emergency room. When he was discharged, they refused to take him back.

All of the placements ended because of alleged abuse in the foster home or because Rick was no longer wanted. Because of this I expected him to have an attachment disorder but when he was 5 a pediatric neurologist diagnosed him as having possible Fetal Alcohol Syndrome and prescribed Ritalin. My medical dictionary and other research didn't tell me much: just that it was a cause of mental retardation. Rick didn't look like the photos and had none of the physical characteristics. I dismissed it. I was in denial. I figured a secure, stable, loving home would work wonders for my Ricky.

The Early Years

Despite his early problems, Rick made progress. Then he seemed to "plateau" and failed to respond to behavior modification techniques or any other attempts to control his destructive behavior. Those important in his life went to great lengths to try to change his impulsivity, his "noncompliance," his inability to learn from his mistakes, and his obsessive verbal perseveration (endless repetition of a given subject). Nothing worked. Others met his failures with increasing hostility.

Our Crisis

At 13, Rick grew to over six feet tall, and was suddenly stronger than me. I had been able to physically prevent him from leaving the house when he was smaller but it became increasingly difficult. When he became angry and was unsupervised in the community, he was dangerous. He was often destructive of property and his impulsive actions threatened himself and others.

> **FAST FACT**
>
> A study in the state of Washington found that children in foster care had a rate of FAS ten to fifteen times higher than in the general population.

The breaking point came one day when, in a rage, he tried to push his way past me to the front door. Simply creating a physical barrier to his bolting no longer worked. He was hardened to physical restraint and more willing to use violence. I could no longer contain him. In desperation, to keep him from hurting others and himself, I grabbed a plastic whiffle bat and tried to keep him at bay by swinging it wildly in front of me. We both ended up with a bloody nose and it was he who called the police. When the patrolman asked me if I wanted him removed, I said "yes." They led my little boy away to a psychiatric ward as a "danger to himself and others." We were both in tears, and he was in handcuffs. I can't imagine parents believing anything other than they had failed.

My Breakthrough

I left my son in confinement and on my way to visit him the next day I bought a book that I had heard mentioned in a newspaper article. It was called *The Broken Cord*. From that book and other materials, I learned for the first time that a newborn doesn't need all the characteristics of FAS to have serious damage from prenatal alcohol exposure. I

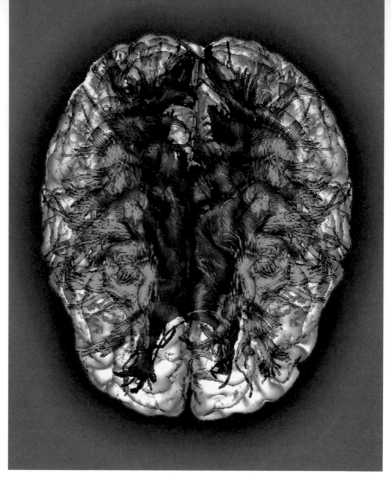

A digital infrared scan of a healthy brain shows white matter nerve fibers in green, blue, and red. Research indicates that FAS damages these areas of the brain. (Zephyr/Photo Researchers, Inc.)

learned that brain and other vital organ damage could be severe even in the absence of a developmental disability. I learned that the executive function of the brain is usually affected by prenatal exposure and the most frequent result of this is lack of impulse control. I discovered one other important thing that had never occurred to me—I was not alone. Reading this important book changed my life. It gave me new insight and a desire to learn more. On a spiritual level it gave meaning to the chaos. It turns out that Rick's confinement was the beginning of a new journey for both of us.

The Real Story

If this were simply the story of a persevering mom hanging in there with an abused kid and overcoming adversity and some of the affects of a traumatic childhood it would make good reading but it wouldn't begin to tell the story. This story is not my story but the story of thousands of kids born each year with brain damage caused by prenatal exposure to alcohol and experiencing the same things.

Experts estimate that 5000 babies are born with Fetal Alcohol Syndrome (FAS) in the United States each year. Who knows how many remain undiagnosed. It's the number one preventable cause of mental retardation in our country. These figures are for FAS alone. An estimated three to ten times this figure have other disorders related to prenatal alcohol exposure. The term now commonly used by researchers and experts to describe everyone affected by maternal drinking is Fetal Alcohol Spectrum Disorders (FASD). FASD is the entire iceberg while FAS is the small tip above the waterline and in full view. A recent study found that approximately one newborn in a hundred has significant damage caused by prenatal alcohol exposure.

Individuals having effects "below the surface" of this iceberg have more problems because that water is murky and it's hard to see. Trouble with the law, substance abuse, disruptive school experiences and mental illness occur at alarming rates in individuals with FASD. Called "secondary disabilities" many of these can be prevented. The most important way to prevent them is by getting appropriate services for those who need them. . . .

The Journey Continues

It has been over a decade since my crisis-producing epiphany, and my son and I have a good relationship. Time is a great healer, and it seems with better understanding and support for Rick much of the emotional damage of those terrible years has been reversed. Rick is a very loving, gentle and humorous young man. I don't take credit for that. It is his natural, God-given nature. He simply needed an opportunity to show it. I am fortunate.

Many parents have far more problems as their child enters adolescence and beyond.

Though I'm a single mom, I had to quit my job as a Special Education teacher and start a business I could do from home. I am one of the lucky parents of a child with a Fetal Alcohol Spectrum Disorder—my son qualifies for services through the regional center system of California. It is sad but true that a protective factor for secondary disabilities caused by FASD is an IQ or overall intelligence score below 70. Those above this amazingly arbitrary number are usually locked out of the service system. This is something we seek to change in California and nationally, as the systems that often end up "treating" our children with FASD are called substance abuse, mental health and criminal justice.

The NineZero Project

As a result of my contacting the Arc of Riverside, telling my story and sharing my knowledge, I was hired on as their FASD coordinator. Thus has begun a new chapter in our continuing journey. The Arc program is called the NineZero Project. It means Nine Months, Zero Alcohol. Coined and trademarked by Arc Riverside, NineZero is understood instantly as an affirmation of total abstinence during pregnancy. . . .

Our youth are the next generation of parents, and we want to create a culture that looks at drinking during pregnancy in the same way that the majority view drinking and driving. It isn't cool and it isn't smart. Think of the disabilities that will not occur in our children and the economic savings to our overburdened medical and social service systems if we lower the incidence of FASD even a few percent! Ricky and I discuss this often as we work with community groups and tell our story. We believe we can be a small part of making this happen. It is our way of giving meaning to our incredible journey.

How FAS Affects Me

David

In the following article fifteen-year-old David shares his story of living with fetal alcohol syndrome (FAS), the most common manifestation of fetal alcohol spectrum disorders (FASD). David understands a lot about his FAS, how it makes him different, and the challenges he faces because of it. However, there are a lot of things David is good at. He likes helping others, and he has a job helping medical students learn about FAS. He wishes that everyone understood FAS. David lives in Canada and contributed his personal story to FASD Connections, an organization devoted to helping those who have FASD.

My name is David and I am 15½ years old and in Grade 8. I have FAS. I have a brother and a sister who also have FAS. I am the oldest. We live together in our family. I was diagnosed with FAS when I was 9 years old. I understand a lot about it.

When I was little, I lived with my birth mother. She had a problem with alcohol and drugs. She did all her life. She did not do this on purpose. I think she had FAS too.

SOURCE: David, "Things I Want People to Know," FASDConnections.ca. Reproduced by permission.

I went to my first foster home when I was a baby. I was in lots of foster homes because my birth mother could not handle us and did not know how to take care of us. Lots of things happened to us. My brother had 3 broken arms in one year and I got a big scar on my forehead. All of us were in different foster homes until the last one. Then we got adopted when I was 9, and my sister was 8 and my brother was 6.

I used to see my birth mother once a month after I got adopted when we would take her out for brunch. She died last December from AIDS and Hepatitis C.

How FAS Affects Me

I am very small for my age. I have always been the smallest kid in my class even though I am the oldest kid in the class. I had to have braces on my teeth because my jaw is too small for my adult teeth to come in properly. I don't feel pain. You can stomp on my toes and it does not hurt at all. It never hurts if I injure myself. People always ask me what it feels like, but I don't know what to tell them.

My fingers are not straight and they go skinny at the tip. My fingernails don't grow hardly at all. My face doesn't look FAS anymore because when you get older and you have FAS, your face changes and you mostly look just like other people.

But this does not mean I can grow out of it. I can't. I have it for the rest of my life.

My brain is smaller than a regular one, so I have a smaller head. I have really big problems with learning all kinds of things. My IQ is 76. I know that means I don't learn like other people do, or as fast.

Things That Challenge Me

Things that are hard for me to do are things like math!!!! It feels like it is impossible for me to do. I have just finally figured out what a loonie and a toonie are—you had to say one dollar or two dollars or else I wouldn't get it. I don't understand how much things cost and get mixed up. I can only sort of tell time on a round clock. I use a digital clock and watch. I cannot figure out "how long [a] time [is]" and need LOTS of help. It is very frustrating for me.

I have a terrible memory!! I forget things all the time. I forget things pretty soon after I learn them. This is very frustrating because I have to learn it again. I forget all kinds of things, like what I just said and where I put something, or what happened a little while ago. *I HATE IT!!!!*

I am a horrible speller!!

I have a really hard time paying attention and I get *VERY* hyper when there is too much going on. It is very hard for me to stay in a classroom. The resource room works better for me because the teacher will sit by me and go step-by-step and explain it my way, simply. It is quieter and has less distractions.

When people talk to me with big words, I don't understand them. You have to use small words and slow down and it takes longer for me to figure out what you mean. Sometimes, I never do. I have to think over what I say too, because sometimes what I said doesn't make sense to me either.

> **FAST FACT**
>
> A 2006 study found that 74 percent of children with FASD were diagnosed as having attention-deficit/hyperactivity disorder.

It is hard for me to get friends and keep them. Kids used to pick on me, and be mean to me a lot in grade school. This year in high school I only went half days until February. Then I went all day for 2 months but now I go half days again because things were not working out. I only took 4 classes—drama, art, Gym and resource room—when I went all day and now I just take Art and Resource Room. School is very hard and not fun.

Things I Am Good At

I am good at gym. I am an excellent swimmer and I am good at diving. We have a pool so I can do this a lot and use up my energy. I am good at outdoor activities and I like to be able to run around.

I am good at making posters for school. I was a good reading tutor to the Grade One student I helped last year. I was also a buddy to a Grade One and Two class. That means I help them with art, stuff on the computer, and I write out the rough copy for them of their journals. I have to set a good example for them of proper behaviour.

I am good at helping with most things as long as I know what I have to do, and I like helping.

I have done excellent science fair reports on FAS. I know a lot about it and I can teach people about it. I help to teach second year medical students every year and have my own groups of them that I talk to by myself, six at a time. I do it two afternoons a week for two months every year. I also do home interviews with third year medical students so they really get to learn about FASD. I am very good at this and I think it is very important to do this. It is an important job.

What I Want People to Understand

What I really want people to understand about me is that I need reminding about most things. I *DO NOT* forget on purpose!! I would never remember to take medicine unless someone told me to no matter even if I was really sick. Actually, I probably wouldn't know I was sick. I need someone (my mom) to go to appointments and meetings and things like that with me. I do not understand what people tell me, especially when they use big words and talk too fast for me. I never understand what the principal is saying to me, and then I can't remember it.

I don't feel pain the same way as other people—I am not too sure what it is supposed to be like. That means I can get sick or hurt and not really know it.

I think I will always need help with how money works. I know I need a trust account so I don't spend all my money and have no food. If I have no food, I will get sick. But I also want to have some money for my own to spend on stuff.

I don't know the difference from 10 minutes to an hour so I need other people to help me so I am not late, too early or forget. I do not get places on time if no one helps me. I would always be late for appointments without someone to tell me when we have to go. That does not mean I am not responsible, just I forget a lot and I can never figure out how much time things take.

Whenever I get frustrated, I explode. It's not because I am a bad person. I am a good person. I have a hard time judging things. Lots of times I make mistakes because I don't understand, no matter how hard I try.

I also won't ask questions, because I don't want to look like an idiot, not because I am not listening to what people say. I need people to be patient with me and to always explain things to someone like my mom so I can have help.

If I Could Have Three Wishes:
• I wish that everyone understood FAS.
• I wish I could get more chances to do the things I am good at, instead of all the things I have so much trouble with, in a school for kids like me with FASD.
• I wish that there were jobs for people with FASD that paid money, and more programs to teach you how to get a job.

If I could have another wish, I would wish for a million dollars so I could build a school for people with FASD and for adults with FASD who quit school because it was too hard.

An Adult Silenced by FAS

Megan Holland

In the following article Megan Holland writes about twenty-year-old Alaskan Justin Scott and the damage his mother's alcohol abuse has caused him. Justin was born with a high level of alcohol in his bloodstream. He does not talk and is cognitively about six years old. However, Justin has a loving adoptive family and receives assistance from many organizations, which help to keep his life full and rich. Holland is a reporter for the *Anchorage Daily News* in Alaska.

Justin Scott sits at his dining room table dabbing pink frosting on a snowman sugar cookie and humming "Silent Night." The chaos of his young niece and nephew decorating their own cookies bubbles around him.

If the 20-year-old could sing to his family, maybe he would. But Justin can't form the words to talk. His best

SOURCE: Megan Holland, "The Adult Face of Fetal Alcohol Syndrome," *Anchorage Daily News*, December 27, 2007. Copyright © 2007, The Anchorage Daily News, a subsidiary of The McClatchy Company. Reproduced by permission.

communication is through jerky motions of American Sign Language.

There are a lot of things Justin can't do.

Many Alaskan Children Have FAS

Developmentally disabled and cognitively about six years old, Justin is an adult face of fetal alcohol syndrome [FAS]. That he has made it this long still awes his adoptive parents, Allan and Cheri Scott. He was considered a "successfully resuscitated miscarriage" on his birth papers when he was born three months early with a .237 blood alcohol level—that's three times the legal limit for an adult driver.

There are hundreds of young people like Justin in Alaska, and thousands more that don't look as if they have suffered damage from their mothers' drinking during pregnancy but show other telltale signs, the invisible disabilities —the poor reasoning and judgment, the hyperactive behaviour, the poor co-ordination.

Alaska has one of the highest rates in the US of fetal alcohol syndrome and fetal alcohol spectrum disorders, an umbrella term that encompasses less severe cases than FAS. The rate in Alaska is five times higher than Arizona, for instance, and four times higher than New York, according to the Centres for Disease Control and Prevention [CDCP]. About 160 infants are born each year in Alaska with FAS or other effects from maternal alcohol use, according to state figures. Part of the reason for this is that Alaska has one of the highest rates of alcoholism in the country.

Justin's biological mother was living in a tent near the Alaska Native Medical Centre when she went into labor and a fellow homeless person told her to go to the nearby hospital. She was so intoxicated that it took her newborn 0.9 kilogram baby four days to dry out [metabolize the alcohol in his system].

Justin was her third child born with effects from her drinking. Justin's older sister would end up in a mental health facility. His other sibling ended up in the care of his mother's family.

Justin's mother visited him while he was in the hospital for the months following his birth but either didn't want him or just couldn't care for him, so the state stepped in. She died when he was about one year old; her stomach hemorrhaged, a complication of her alcoholism.

Adopted by His Foster Family

The Scotts took in Justin when he was just a baby. They were a medical foster family and had dealt with tough situations before. When he was three years old, they adopted him into their family of four—Cheri, Allan, and their two biological children, teenagers at the time.

At first, taking care of Justin meant waking up every two hours to feed him. But with time, the Scotts learned to continue with their lives—with Justin always near them, literally. When the Scotts take their Harley Davidson for a spin, Justin sits in a sidecar.

Back in the dining room of his home, Justin and his niece, nine-year-old Rosebud, and his nephew, four-year-old Curtis, listen to Cheri, a woman who strikes one as the type born to be a mum, with a soft voice and seemingly endless patience. She helps them choose among the different shaped cookies, including the Christmas tree, the candy cane or the airplane.

Later, Justin will eat his dinner and take his shower before going to bed, but for now, this is the family fun.

"Oh, Justin, you got a letter from Crystal!" Cheri says, getting right up close to Justin so he can see her in his vision, which is limited to about two feet away.

She hands him the printed letter, highlighted in fluorescent pink. He looks at her and a smile crosses his face.

> **FAST FACT**
>
> The state of Alaska's FAS Surveillance Project estimates that approximately fifteen children with FAS are born in Alaska each year.

He signs the word for "soft" using both hands. "Soft" is Justin's way of saying he likes something.

Crystal is Justin's girlfriend, a 32-year-old woman with FAS who is cognitively about the same age as him. They met at an FAS camp three years ago. The pair see each other about twice a year and correspond often, both sets of parents helping them communicate. Their affection is usually limited to holding hands but once Justin did kiss her on the top of her head, Cheri said.

Justin takes the letter and brings it close to his face to read, moving his head as he reads the lines. His joy is easy to see.

"For us, we feel so lucky that they found each other," Cheri says. "They want a friend."

Justin has learned to read and type through his Alternative Career Education program with the Anchorage School District, designed to help children like him to learn life skills. When he turns 22, Justin will transition from spending his days at school to a state-funded adult program through the Division of Vocational Rehabilitation.

Justin (pictured), who is afflicted with FAS, has many developmental problems, including severe vision impairment. (**Bill Roth/MCT/Landov**)

Caring for Justin Is Not Always Easy

Living with FAS has drastically changed the lives of the Scotts. Cheri admits it hasn't been easy and often means she is taking care of Justin and not herself. But she's also learned a lot from her sensitive son, she says. He taught her not to raise her voice, and to treat others with kindness; if she doesn't, he senses it and will cry.

"People treat him differently. They are gentle with him," says his father, Allan. "I think he brings that out in people."

In Alaska, 14 per cent of women of childbearing age had been binge drinking within a month of a 2005 study, according to the CDCP.

The total lifetime cost of providing services to an individual with FAS is estimated at $US3.1 million. That includes medical costs, therapies and residential care. In 20 years, Justin has had 22 operations.

The Scotts are assisted by the state and local charities, including the care of Catholic Social Services, which has been helping with Justin since 1987. The organisation provides caregivers for Justin. With them, he swims at the Alaska Club, eats at the Village Inn and visits the Imaginarium. During the school year, caregivers spend about 15 hours a week with him. During the summer, they spend about 40.

Caring for Justin costs the nonprofit about $US40,000 a year. The money to pay for the care comes from Medicaid, grants, and donations.

Cheri says if she could have one wish come true it would be to give her son a voice. She has a recurring dream in which Justin walks into her bedroom and says "Hi Mum," and just starts talking. But for now, the sound of him humming "Silent Night" gives her the joy she craves from her son.

GLOSSARY

alcoholism   A chronic, progressive, and potentially fatal disorder caused by both genetic and environmental factors. It is characterized by tolerance and physical dependence, manifested by the inability to control drinking behavior. It is often accompanied by diverse personality changes and social consequences.

alcohol-related birth defects (ARBD)   A term coined by the Institute of Medicine in 1996 and used to describe individuals with confirmed maternal alcohol use and one or more congenital defects, including heart, bone, kidney, vision, or hearing abnormalities.

alcohol-related neurodevelop- mental disorder (ARND)   A term coined by the Institute of Medicine in 1996 to describe individuals with confirmed maternal alcohol use, nerve-development abnormalities, and a complex pattern of behavioral or cognitive abnormalities inconsistent with developmental level and not explained by genetic background or environment.

alcohol screening   A question-based method for identifying individuals with alcohol problems and assessing the severity of use.

binge drinking   Refers to the consumption of four or more drinks in about two hours.

birth defect   A physical or biochemical defect (e.g., Down syndrome, FAS, cleft palate) that is present at birth and may be inherited or environmentally induced.

congenital defects   Physical imperfections with which a person is born, acquired during development in the uterus. The defects may be due to genetics or to fetal injury or insult (e.g., maternal alcohol use or infection). Infants with an FASD may be born with congenital defects (e.g., heart defects, limb and joint abnormalities).

developmental disabilities   A diverse group of physical, cognitive, psychological, sensory, and speech impairments that begin any time during development up to eighteen years of age.

dysmorphology   A term coined by David W. Smith for the study of human congenital malformations. A dysmorphologist is a clinician who specializes in this field.

epicanthal folds   Skin folds covering the inner corners of the eyes; an indication of fetal alcohol syndrome.

failure to thrive   A term used to describe children early in life who do not receive or are unable to take in or retain adequate nutrition to gain weight and grow as expected. Often, children with FAS are initially diagnosed with failure to thrive.

fetal alcohol spectrum disorder (FASD)   An umbrella term describing the range of effects that can occur in an individual whose mother drank alcohol during pregnancy. These effects may include physical, mental, behavioral, and/or learning disabilities with possible lifelong implications. The term is not intended for use as a clinical diagnosis.

fetal alcohol syndrome (FAS)   A term coined in 1973 by Kenneth Jones and David Smith at the University of Washington to describe individuals with documented prenatal exposure to alcohol and (1) prenatal and postnatal growth retardation, (2) characteristic facial features, and (3) central nervous system problems.

fetus — A developing being, usually from three months after conception until birth for humans. Prior to that time, the developing being is typically referred to as an embryo.

heavy drinking — Generally refers to the consumption of five or more drinks on the same occasion on five or more days in the past month. Heavy drinking during pregnancy can result in an FASD.

learning disabilities — Difficulties with reading, writing, spelling, computing, or communication.

mental retardation — A disorder characterized by a significantly below-average score on a test of intellectual ability and limitations in such areas as self-direction, school, work, leisure activities, daily living, and social and communication skills. About 27 percent of individuals with FAS and 9 percent with fetal alcohol effects meet intelligence quotient (IQ) criteria for mental retardation (a score of 70 or below).

microcephaly — A congenital anomaly of the central nervous system in which the head circumference is more than three standard deviations below the mean for age and sex.

philtrum — The vertical groove between the nose and the middle part of the upper lip. Individuals diagnosed with FAS have a flattening of the philtrum.

postnatal — Refers to events occurring after birth.

prenatal — Refers to events existing or occurring before birth.

standard drink — One standard drink is 12 ounces of beer, 5 ounces of wine, or 1.5 ounce of hard liquor. All have the same equivalency of 0.48 ounces of pure alcohol.

teratogen   Any substance, such as alcohol, or condition, such as measles, that can cause damage to a fetus, resulting in deformed bodily structures.

trimester   A three-month period during pregnancy. Pregnancy is divided into three trimesters.

CHRONOLOGY

B.C. **1380–1050** In the biblical book of Judges it is recorded that an angel spoke to the mother of Samson and said, "Thou shalt conceive, and bear a son. Now therefore, beware, I pray thee, and drink not wine nor strong drink" (Judges 13:3–4).

A.D. **1725** During the English "gin epidemic," the Royal College of Physicians reports that parental drinking is a cause of "weak, feeble and distempered children."

1834 A report to the British House of Commons says infants born to alcoholic mothers sometimes have a "starved, shriveled, and imperfect look."

1899 English prison physician William Sullivan notes that pregnant alcoholic female prisoners have higher rates of stillbirth than their sober female relatives, and he suggests that alcohol is the cause.

Early 1900s Experimental studies of the effects of prenatal alcohol exposure in animals shows delayed growth, physical malformations, and high mortality.

1968 Frenchman Paul Lemoine publishes a clinical description of 127 children born to predominantly alcoholic mothers and notes physical malformations, developmental delays, and behavioral problems.

1973 American dysmorphologists Kenneth Jones and David Smith of the University of Washington Medical School coin the term "fetal alcohol syndrome."

1973–1985	Almost two thousand articles on FAS are published in professional journals.
1981	The U.S. surgeon general recommends warnings against alcohol use during pregnancy.
1988	The U.S. Congress passes the Alcoholic Beverage Labeling Act, which requires alcoholic beverage labels to carry a warning about birth defects.
1996	The U.S. Institute of Medicine coins the terms "alcohol-related birth defects (ARBD)" and "alcohol-related neurodevelopmental disorder (ARND)."
2005	The U.S. surgeon general issues an advisory that pregnant women should not drink alcohol during pregnancy.

ORGANIZATIONS TO CONTACT

The editors have compiled the following list of organizations concerned with the issues debated in this book. The descriptions are derived from materials provided by the organizations. All have publications or information available for interested readers. The list was compiled on the date of publication of the present volume; the information provided here may change. Be aware that many organizations take several weeks or longer to respond to inquiries, so allow as much time as possible for the receipt of requested materials.

American College of Obstetricians and Gynecologists (ACOG)
409 Twelfth St. SW
Washington, DC
20090-6920
(202) 638-5577
Web site:
www.acog.org

The ACOG is a nonprofit organization of professionals who provide health care for women. The ACOG advocates for quality health care for women, promotes patient education, and increases awareness among its members and the public of the changing issues facing women's health care. The ACOG issues important guidelines and bulletins and publishes several journals, including *Obstetrics & Gynecology* and *Special Issues in Women's Health*.

FASD Center for Excellence Substance Abuse & Mental Health Services Administration (SAMHSA).
1 Choke Cherry Rd.
Rockville, MD 20857
866-STOPFAS
(786-7327)
Web site: www.fasd center.samhsa.gov

SAMHSA, part of the U.S. Department of Health and Human Services, is the lead federal agency addressing substance abuse and mental health services. The SAMHSA FASD Center for Excellence was launched in 2001. The mission of the center is to facilitate the development and improvement of prevention, treatment, and care systems in the United States by providing national leadership and facilitating collaboration in the field. The goals of the center are to reduce the number of infants born who are prenatally exposed to alcohol, increase functioning of persons who have an FASD, and improve quality of life for individuals and families affected by FASD. The center has developed a number of publications, including the *FASD: Knot Alone* newsletters, information on the cost of FASD, and specific reports.

FAS Family Resource Institute
PO Box 2525
Lynnwood, WA 98036
Web site: www.fetal alcoholsyndrome.org

The mission of the FAS Family Resource Institute, a nonprofit educational organization, is to identify, understand, and care for people with FASD and their families. Additionally, the FAS Family Resource Institute seeks to prevent future generations from having to live with FAS. Up until 2008, the organization published the *FAS Times*, a newsletter. The FASD Family Preservation blog is available at http://fasblog.fetalalcoholsyndrome .org.

Fetal Alcohol Disorders Society
2448 Hamilton Rd.
Bright's Grove, ON
Canada N0N 1C0
(519) 869-8026
Web site: www.faslink .org

The Fetal Alcohol Disorders Society is a nonprofit organization formed by a group of parents who were struggling with the lack of professional knowledge and support in the fetal alcohol spectrum disorders (FASD) field. The Fetal Alcohol Disorders Society Web site serves as a clearinghouse of FASD-related information.

National Center on Birth Defects and Developmental Disabilities Centers for Disease Control and Prevention (CDC)
1600 Clifton Rd., MS E-86, Atlanta, GA 30333
(800) 232-4636
Web site: www.cdc .gov/ncbddd/fasd/ index.html

The National Center on Birth Defects and Developmental Disabilities, part of the CDC, is dedicated to helping people with birth defects and disabilities live life to the fullest. The mission of the CDC FAS Prevention Team is to prevent fetal alcohol syndrome and other prenatal alcohol-related conditions and to ameliorate these conditions in children already affected. Its Web site provides information on a variety of topics, including FASD. The CDC provides brochures, fact sheets, training guides, data, and statistics on FASD.

The Guttmacher Institute
1301 Connecticut Ave. NW, Ste. 700
Washington, DC 20036
(202) 296-4012
toll-free: (877) 823-0262
fax: (202) 223-5756
Web site: www.guttmacher.org

The Guttmacher Institute advances sexual and reproductive health in the United States and worldwide through an interrelated program of social science research, policy analysis, and public education designed to generate new ideas, encourage enlightened public debate, promote sound policy and program development, and inform individual decision-making. The institute produces a wide range of publications, including *Perspectives on Sexual and Reproductive Health, International Perspectives on Sexual and Reproductive Health,* and the *Guttmacher Policy Review.*

March of Dimes Birth Defects Foundation
1275 Mamaroneck Ave., White Plains NY 10605
(914) 428-7100
fax: (914) 428-8203
Web site: www .marchofdimes.com

The March of Dimes is one of the oldest U.S. organizations devoted to improving the health of babies. It raises money to help prevent birth defects, such as fetal alcohol syndrome, genetic disorders, premature births, and infant deaths. The March of Dimes carries out its mission through research, community service, education, and advocacy. The organization publishes a monthly e-newsletter called *Miracles.*

National Association for Children of Alcoholics (NACoA)
11426 Rockville Pike Ste. 301, Rockville MD 20852
(301) 468-0985
toll-free: (888) 55-4COAS
fax: 301-468-0987
e-mail: nacoa@ nacoa.org
Web site: www .nacoa.org

The NACoA is a national nonprofit organization working on behalf of children of alcohol- and drug-dependent parents. The association works to raise public awareness; provide leadership in public policy at the national, state, and local levels; advocate for appropriate, effective, and accessible education and prevention services; and facilitate and advance professional knowledge and understanding of this issue. The NACoA publishes a newsletter, *Network,* and several guides for parents and teens.

National Institute for Alcohol Abuse and Alcoholism (NIAAA)
5635 Fishers Ln.
MSC 9304, Bethesda
MD 20892-9304
(301) 443-3860
Web site: www.ni
aaa.nih.gov

The NIAAA, a branch of the National Institutes of Health, is the U.S. agency charged with reducing alcohol-related problems through supporting research, disseminating findings, and collaborating with other institutions, nationally and internationally. The NIAAA publications include *Alcohol Alert* and *Alcohol Research and Health*.

National Organization on Fetal Alcohol Syndrome (NOFAS)
1200 Eton Ct. NW
3rd Fl., Washington
DC 20007
(202) 785-4585
fax: (202) 466-6456
e-mail: information
@nofas.org
Web site: www
.nofas.org

The NOFAS is an international nonprofit organization committed solely to FASD primary prevention, advocacy, and support. NOFAS works to increase public awareness and mobilize grassroots action in diverse communities. The organization represents the interests of persons with FASD and their caregivers as the liaison to researchers and policy makers. The NOFAS strives to reduce the stigma and improve the quality of life for affected individuals and families. The NOFAS clearinghouse provides information, resources, referrals, and materials on alcohol and pregnancy, and fetal alcohol spectrum disorders.

Teratology Society
1821 Michael Faraday
Dr., Ste. 300, Reston
VA 20190
(703) 438-3104
fax: (703) 438-3113
e-mail: tshq@
teratology.org
Web site: http://
teratology.org

The Teratology Society was formed in 1960 to foster the exchange of information relating to congenital (birth) defects, including their nature, cause, mechanism, and prevention. *Birth Defects Research* (formerly known as *Teratology*) is the official journal of the society. It is a three-part journal that publishes animal, clinical, and experimental research papers as well as reviews and other pertinent material relating to congenital malformations.

FOR FURTHER READING

Books

Elizabeth Armstrong, *Conceiving Risk, Bearing Responsibility: Fetal Alcohol Syndrome & the Diagnosis of Moral Disorder*. Baltimore: Johns Hopkins University Press, 2003.

Beverley Brenna, *The Moon Children*. Markham, ON: Red Deer, 2007.

Bonnie Buxton, *Damaged Angels: An Adoptive Mother's Struggle to Understand the Tragic Toll of Alcohol in Pregnancy*. Jackson, TN: Da Capo, 2005.

Jody Allen Crowe, *The Fatal Link: The Connection Between School Shooters and the Brain Damage from Exposure to Alcohol*. Denver: Outskirts, 2009.

Michael Dorris, *The Broken Cord*. New York: Harper-Perennial, 1990.

Janet Golden, *Message in a Bottle: The Making of Fetal Alcohol Syndrome*. Cambridge, MA: Harvard University Press, 2005.

Judith Kleinfeld, *Fantastic Antone Grows Up*. Fairbanks: University of Alaska Press, 2000.

Jodee and Liz Kulp, *The Best I Can Be*. Brooklyn Park, MN: Better Endings New Beginnings, 2009.

Kieran O'Malley, *ADHD and Fetal Alcohol Spectrum Disorders (FASD)*. Hauppauge, NY: Nova, 2007.

Jennifer Salmon, *Fetal Alcohol Syndrome: New Zealand Birth Mothers' Experiences*. Wellington, NZ: Dunmore, 2005.

Rickie Solinger, *Pregnancy and Power: A Short History of Reproductive Politics in America*. New York: New York University Press, 2005.

Ann Pytkowicz Streissguth, *Fetal Alcohol Syndrome: A Guide for Families and Communities*. Baltimore: Brookes, 1997.

Ann Streissguth and Jonathan Kanter, *The Challenge of Fetal Alcohol Syndrome: Overcoming Secondary Disabilities*. Seattle: University of Washington Press, 1997.

Morasha Winokur, *My Invisible World: Life with My Brother, His Disability and His Dog*. Brooklyn Park, MN: Better Endings New Beginnings, 2009.

Periodicals   Jill U. Adams, "Alcohol, Coffee and Baby," *Los Angeles Times*, November 10, 2008.

Doug Brunk, "Should Fetal Alcohol Spectrum Disorder Be Included in DSM-V?" *Clinical Psychiatry News*, August, 2009.

Linda Carroll, "Alcohol's Toll on Fetuses: Even Worse than Thought," *New York Times*, November 4, 2003.

GP, "Behind the Headlines: Can Exposure in the Womb Leave a Taste for Alcohol?" March 20, 2009.

Robert B. Hopkins et al. "Universal or Targeted Screening for Fetal Alcohol Exposure: A Cost-Effectiveness Analysis," *Journal of Studies on Alcohol and Drugs*, July 2008.

Tracy Johnson, "Project Sheds Light on Disability Born of Alcohol: Afflicted at Risk of Trouble with the Legal System," *Seattle Post-Intelligencer*, April 5, 2005.

Marguerite Kelly, "Fetal Alcohol Syndrome's Long-Lasting Impression," *Washington Post*, November 27, 2009.

Barry Lester, Lynne Andreozzi, and Lindsey Appiah, "Substance Use During Pregnancy: Time for Policy to Catch Up with Research," *Harm Reduction Journal*, April 2004.

Paul Masotti et al. "Preventing Fetal Alcohol Spectrum Disorder in Aboriginal Communities: A Methods Development Project," *PLoS Medicine*, January 10, 2006.

Julia Moskin, "The Weighty Responsibility of Drinking for Two," *New York Times*, November 29, 2006.

OB/GYN Clinical Alert, "The Effect of Maternal Alcohol Consumption on Fetal Growth and Preterm Birth," April 1, 2009.

Mary O'Connor, "Preconception Care for Reducing Alcohol Exposure in Pregnancy," *Female Patient*, October 2008.

William Stewart, "'Drunk' and Disorderly: The Children Damaged While Still in the Womb," *Times Educational Supplement* (London), May 29, 2009.

Daniel Wattendorf and Maximilian Muenke, "Fetal Alcohol Spectrum Disorders," *American Family Physician*, July 15, 2005.

Women's Health Weekly, "Genetics Can Mediate Vulnerability to Alcohol's Effects During Pregnancy, May 7, 2009.

Internet Sources

Juju Chang, Mable Chan, and Olivia Sterns, "Can Pregnant Women Drink Alcohol in Moderation?" ABC News, February 2, 2008. http://abcnews.go.com/Health/OnCall/Story?id=4232695&page=1.

Tom Robertson and Cara Hetland, "Is There Justice for People with Fetal Alcohol Brain Damage?" Minnesota

Public Radio, December 20, 2007. http://minnesota.pub
licradio.org/display/web/2007/12/18/fasdjuducial.

Science Daily, "Children with Fetal Alcohol Spectrum
Disorders (FASD) Have More Severe Behavioral Problems than Children with Attention Deficit Hyperactivity
Disorder (ADHD), Study Finds," July 20, 2009. www
.sciencedaily.com/releases/2009/07/090716164335.htm.

Daniel Vance, "Fetal Alcohol Disorder Often Mistaken
for Other Ailments," *New Bern (NC) Sun Journal*, February 14, 2010. www.newbernsj.com/articles/disorder-
66893-fetal-alcohol.html.

INDEX

A

Adams, Monica, 37–40

Adults, impact of FAS on, 20, 32–40

Alaska, number of children born with FAS annually, 110

Alcohol
  consumption in Russia, 9–10
  effects on fetal mice, genetic role in, *24*
  effects on fetus, 18, 28, 39, 62
  first identified as teratogen, 75
  genes may determine sensitivity to maternal exposure to, 22–26
  prevalence of pregnant women using, 50, *56*, 57, *68*
  use by women aged 18–44, *51*
  use by women of childbearing age, 25, *63*
  women abusing, FAS prevention should focus on helping, 74–80

Alcohol Policy Information System, 81

Alcohol-exposed pregnancy (AEP), 70
  role of physicians in preventing, *71*, 71–73
  states having provisions in child welfare proceedings for, *82*

Alcoholism
  in Alaska, 109
  in Russia, 10
  among women, 67, 75

Alcohol-related neurodevelopmental disorder (ARND), 16, 20, 82

American College of Obstetricians and Gynecologists, 29, 64

American Pregnancy Association, 50

Apoptosis, 29

Attention-deficit/hyperactivity disorder (ADHD), 19
  percent of children with FASD diagnosed with, 105

Australia, alcohol use by pregnant women in, 55–57

Australian National Health and Medical Research Council, 55

B

Balachova, Tatiana, 10–11

Behavioral problems, 16, 23
  can be addressed by early diagnosis/intervention, 21
  of FASD are often attributed to other causes, 42–43

Benedict XVI (pope), 68

β-nicotinamide adenine dinucleotide, 28

Binge drinking, 17
  defined for women, 70
  by pregnant women in first trimester, 78

Biological Psychiatry (journal), 23